THE LAST
SHEPHERDS

D0413282

Also by Charles Bowden

The Last Horsemen

THE LAST SHEPHERDS

A VANISHING WAY OF LIFE ON BRITAIN'S TRADITIONAL HILL FARMS

CHARLES BOWDEN

ANDRE
DEUTSCH

The Last Shepherds is a Tyne Tees Television Production

This edition published in 2011
by André Deutsch
an imprint of the Carlton Publishing Group
20 Mortimer Street
London W1T 3JW

First published in 2004
In association with Granada Media Group

Text copyright © Granada Media Group Ltd, 2004

ISBN 978 0 233 00324 5

The publishers would like to thank the following sources for their kind permission to reproduce the pictures in this book:

Picture Section 1
Private Collection/page 1 top, 4, 5
Lee Sutterby/Page 1 bottom, 2, 3, 6, 7, 8

Picture Section 2
Beamish Museum/ 6, 7, 8
Private Collection/page 1, 2, 3, 4 top
Sutcliffe Gallery/ 4 bottom, 5 bottom

Typeset by E-Type, Liverpool

Printed and bound by CPI Group (UK) Ltd, Croydon, CR0 4YY

Contents

Acknowledgements

*T*his book has been written to accompany the CBTV Media/Tyne Tees Television series The *Last Shepherds* and the first people I must thank are the shepherds I worked with while filming the programmes: Dave Baxter, Stewart Wallace and Gwen Wallace. Filming is fun, but it can be a slow and repetitive process at times. They showed great patience as we strove to capture the finer points of sheep and shepherding. My gratitude is also extended to their employers, Mary Carruthers, Judith Ridley and Buccleugh Estates, who kindly gave us permission to bring our cameras onto their farms, and to Robert McKay, Lesley Anderson and Matthew Ridley, who we also filmed on various occasions as part of the series.

Thanks too to the organisers of Rothbury Traditional Music Festival, Alwinton Show, Harbottle Shepherds' Supper and Flotterton Sheepdog Trials for allowing us to film their activities.

Two creative talents I have worked with for a number of years are cameraman Lee Sutterby and film editor Dave Hindmarsh. Both played a huge part in making *The Last Shepherds* such a watchable television series. Lee also took many of the photographs in this book. It was a pleasure, as always, to work with them.

Graeme Thompson, managing director of Tyne Tees Television,

had confidence in this, my latest 'Last of The Line' projects, and my thanks go to him for commissioning the series.

To the following I'm also indebted: Peter Dawson, for pictures of life in Coquetdale in times past; Andrew Morton, Oliver Allison and Frank Wales, for their assistance on Shepherds' Guides; Maurice Reed, for the story of Bellingham Auction Mart; Trevor Simpson, for background on sheep sales; Tom Cowan, for information about quad bikes; Edgar Charlton, for sharing his memories of shepherding in the North Tyne valley; Lt. Col. Richard Cross, for the history of the Otterburn Ranges; Scott Smith, Derek Scrimgeour, Viv Billingham, Raymond MacPherson and David Ogilvie for guidance on sheepdog trials; Liz Ambler and Colin MacGregor at the British Wool Marketing Board for providing facts about wool; Andrew Miller and Albert Weir at Northumberland National Park; Aileen McFadzean, of the Blackface Sheep Breeders' Association; Ian Jones at BAGMA, for data on ATVs; Brian Jeffrey, for advice on veterinary matters; Arthur Rundle, at the Golden Shears World Council; and Michael Shaw, of the Sutcliffe Gallery in Whitby, North Yorkshire.

Readers can contact Wilf Laidler for information about the Border Stick Dressers' Association by email. The address is wilf@wlaidler.freeserve.co.uk and details of *Up the Valley*, Lorna Laidler's book about the Coquet valley in the 1940s, are available on the same site. My thanks to Wilf for also providing information about the population of the Coquet Valley in the 1800s.

Another book I found useful was *Daft Laddies* by Clive Dalton and Don Clegg (email address: donaldclegg@btopenworld.com).

Staff at Beamish Museum in County Durham were extremely helpful, particularly John Gall, Rosemary Allen, Jim Lawson and Carolyn Ware.

My thanks go to my editor, Lorna Russell, at Carlton Books, for guiding me as *The Last Shepherds* developed and grew, and to Rosie Boyle at Granada for her help.

I value the conversations about farm life in the 1920s which I had with my father, John Bowden, who is now in his nineties. He worked as a farm labourer in Northumberland from 1925 to 1935, before renting a farm, and his vivid memories of that era were extremely useful.

Lastly, my thanks to Elspeth, my wife, for the encouragement and support she unfailingly gives me.

Author's Note

Red Sky at night
Shepherds' delight
Red Sky in the morning
Shepherds' warning

Over the last 50 years the face of rural Britain has changed dramatically. Unusual crops, like oilseed rape, linseed and evening primrose, have started to appear. Continental breeds of livestock, led by Charolais cattle and Texel sheep, have pushed aside our native breeds. Farming has become 'pharming' as new treatments for animal ailments have been introduced by drug companies. The tractor and combine harvester have supplanted the horse, the binder and the threshing machine. And the drift from the land, which began with the Industrial Revolution and was exacerbated by two world wars, has continued remorselessly.

As the pace of change has accelerated the desire to make a record of what was happening in the countryside before the old ways of life – and some of the old characters – disappeared altogether has grown. Historians have recorded rural reminiscences on audio tape; publishers have been putting out books full of intriguing old photographs; and as for me, being a television producer, I turned to film. Over three years between 1998 and 2001 cameramen working with me compiled more than 30 hours of footage as we recorded life on one of the very few farms where work-horses are still used. The result was a series of programmes, commissioned by Tyne Tees Television and shown on ITV, together with a video and a book. We called the project *The Last Horsemen.*

The horsemen in question were John Dodd, aged 75, and his 50-year-old son-in-law, David Wise. At their farm in south-west Northumberland all the work is done by six huge Clydesdales. In the winter months they spend long days preparing the land, using horses yoked to a single plough which turns the soil in the time-honoured way. In the spring, horse-drawn drills sow the crops. Summer sees the men riding on an array of ancient hay-making machines. And in the autumn, barley, turnips and potatoes are harvested, using equipment which went out of favour before the Second World War.

One of the horsemen's chief interests is going to auctions at farms where the owner is selling up. These events are like the car boot sales of the agricultural world. Bargains are to be had for old horse-drawn machinery, so long as – like John – you bide your time. For a farmer of his years and experience, that's never a problem.

The programmes stirred memories in a wide range of people. We filmed a horse and cart leading out manure in January, the animal's heavy feet crunching the frozen ground. We captured the horsemen picking stones from a field. And we saw how they trained a young horse, Sandy. For some viewers, these were scenes they hadn't witnessed for more than half a century. Many said it was the sounds of horses working, as much as the pictures that brought it all back. Among the many missives the postman pushed through John Dodd's letterbox was one from New Zealand addressed to 'The Last Horsemen, Northumberland,

England'. To their credit, the people in the sorting office in the nearby town knew where to deliver it. John's fame has spread far.

Guidance about the technical details of working with heavy horses came in part from my father, who worked with horses as a young farm labourer in the 1920s. And it was he who planted the seeds for my next venture. He remembered spending days as a boy watching the comings and goings in the fishing village of Craster on the Northumberland coast and wondered what had happened to cobles, the tiny boats the fishermen used. I decided to find out. With the help of the Coble and Keelboat Society and two local historians, Adrian Osler and Gloria Wilson, I put together *The Last Fishermen*, a series about Britain's few remaining coble fishermen. As was the case with *The Last Horsemen*, it was commissioned by Tyne Tees Television.

Thought to have been pioneered by the Vikings, cobles are wooden boats about 30 feet long. Until the 1930s they relied on sail. With a high bow, flat floor and low stern they're designed to be launched through surf off the sandy beaches and rocky harbours that dot the north-east coast. A century ago, thousands of these small craft were based in ports from Berwick to Scarborough and some writers even called the area the 'coble coast'. But numbers have declined sharply since the Second World War.

In a small boatyard in Whitby I discovered two craftsmen who were working on the first coble to be constructed for a dozen years or more. This was a unique opportunity to record skills which may soon be gone for ever, and we filmed them over a period of nine months as the lovely lines of the boat took shape. While we were in Whitby we went out fishing for cod on *Carisma*, a coble owned by Shaun Elwick, one of the last fishermen to still use long lines baited with thousands of hooks. And at Alnmouth in Northumberland, we filmed Main Stephenson on his coble *Northern Pride* as he went fishing for sea trout using the ancient practice of beach netting. In 2003, when the programmes were transmitted, both skippers were determined to continue fishing, although their incomes were lower than they had been in years gone by. But since then further changes in fishing policy have cast a shadow over what they do. They may well be the last of the line.

Both being reliant on the weather, fishing and farming have their similarities. And I turned back to farming in 2003 to record another disappearing way of life before, once again, it was too late.

Shepherds are becoming something of an endangered species: their numbers are falling rapidly. Mountain districts where there was once a shepherd on every hill are now ranched by one man and his bike. In one valley in the Scottish Borders, the number of shepherds has tumbled from 30 to two in just 20 years. Not only that, the average age of those who are left is going up and there is concern about where the next generation will come from. Some training colleges that used to offer courses on sheep management have dropped them, and those that still run them have suffered a fall in applications. As for filling vacancies on farms, the situation is worst in the remoter regions of Britain, where it's becoming increasingly difficult to get shepherds to stay. There may be benefits in living off the beaten track: the beauty of the surroundings, no neighbours to worry about and plenty of space for exercising the dogs. But being a long way from shops, garages, pubs and cinemas can be frustrating. And for shepherds with children, schools are usually many miles away and are often under threat of closure.

As Stewart Wallace, one of the shepherds who was filmed for

our TV series, says: 'There aren't many young shepherds coming into the job now. Few families want to live "out bye", away from it all. We're 20 miles from the nearest supermarket, ten miles away from the nearest petrol supply. Young shepherds don't want to travel that distance now, especially if they're married. They'd rather be near a town where the wife can find work. I was born and bred out bye. I've never known anything different. But the next generation aren't so keen on being so cut off.'

Stewart's words are echoed by another of the shepherds we filmed, Dave Baxter. 'People will always be needed to look after sheep,' he says. 'But where they're going to get them from I don't know. Very few young ones are being trained.'

One academic suggested to me that young men and women brought up in cities might be lured into the countryside by the romantic notion of working alone on the hills. They would fill the gaps left by shepherds when they retire, he argued. But there is little evidence of such an exodus. If anything, young people are ignoring their rural roots and heading in the opposite direction.

Rural depopulation is not something new, of course. Nor are the problems of living in isolated areas confined to Britain. In large areas of Australia, for instance, young women have all but disappeared from remote farming communities. In 2001, a group of 12 sheep shearers from the Australian outback stripped naked for a calendar in a desperate bid to find wives. The men were praying that by emulating the Women's Institute members from North Yorkshire, who bared all to raise money for cancer research, they would entice women back. It was a forlorn hope.

Meanwhile, as the elder statesmen of the shepherding fraternity die out, so do many of their customs. Where are the sociable get-togethers they used to have at hill-top inns in the North of

England, where stray sheep gathered from the moors were handed back to their rightful owners? The identification marks on their horns and ears had to be checked in the local *Shepherds' Guide*, the flockmaster's Bible which listed every farmer in the district together with illustrations of his sheeps' marks. These 'meets' culminated in a good feed and plenty of drink. They were a much-valued opportunity for shepherds to renew friendships and exchange bits of gossip. But since the foot and mouth epidemic of 2001 they have fallen by the wayside.

With fewer shepherds, what's the future for all the other rural skills and traditions? How much longer will events like 'herds' suppers be held? Will sheepdog trials, classes for 'pack' sheep at local shows, the ability to 'dress' sheep for sales and the art of carving crooks continue? Who will still be writing dialect poetry and composing folk music? It's these vanishing customs and the people who kept them alive that we depict in *The Last Shepherds*. It's a series of programmes, accompanied by this book, about a traditional lifestyle which is under threat from the modern world.

No one can illustrate this better than the figure of Dave Baxter, a shepherd for five decades and one of the North's top sheepdog handlers. I've known Dave for many years, having met him when I was agricultural editor of the *Newcastle Journal*. Approaching the end of his long career, Dave has embraced many of what he would term the 'newfangled' aspects of shepherding, such as the latest medicines, pregnancy-scanning of ewes and quad bikes for transport. But he's also able to recall the Golden Age for shepherds back in the 1950s.

Dave is one of the characters of the hills, happy in his own company but full of wry humour when he's with his colleagues. Uniquely among the shepherds I know, he still fashions his own sheepdog whistles, using scraps of old tin. He argues that they suit him better than those bought from a supplier. But they're also a reminder of the days when shepherds' wages were so low it was sensible to use a home-made whistle rather than fork out a couple of hard-earned shillings for a manufactured one.

Dave has spent all his life on farms in the Cheviot Hills in Northumberland and I decided I would include two other shepherds from the area in my series. They are unusual in that they are a shepherd and a shepherdess – who are also husband and wife. Gwen and Stewart Wallace got to know each other while working side by side on one of the remotest hill farms in the area. Love blossomed, they got engaged and within a year they were married. That was 15 years ago. They complement each other in their work; they are a team. While Welsh-born Gwen has her eye on the future – she's happy working on the computer and emailing her friends in the sheepdog world – Stewart, a Scot, is loth to forget the past. An avid reader, he's interested in the history of the sheep farms in the valley where they live and enjoys running a sheepdog trial. Being an enthusiast for tradition he's also revived the local 'Shepherds' Supper', a pre-lambing time 'hooley' which had folded in recent years through lack of support.

It shouldn't be overlooked that the future for shepherds depends on the prosperity of their employers. Farming has suffered some colossal knocks in recent years – plummeting incomes, BSE and foot and mouth disease – and the industry faces the prospect of more disruption in the years to come. The Government is in the process of changing the way subsidies are distributed. Since 1940 farmers have been encouraged by grants to produce more food, and now they are being told to produce less but to farm in a more environmentally-friendly way. This will mean keeping fewer sheep – with the inevitable knock-on effect of fewer jobs.

Such predictions may be pooh-poohed by some, but the conclusion is inescapable: the people featured in this book may indeed become The Last Shepherds.

Introduction

❧

Keeping Watch

*A*s old as the hills? It may be straining things too far, but shepherds have been around for a long, long time. No one knows exactly when man first tamed wild sheep and gathered them into groups to provide him and his family with sustenance and clothing, but there is archaeological evidence to suggest that shepherds were tending their animals in the remote hills of what is now Turkey as long as 10,000 years ago.

Anyone familiar with the Bible will recognise its opening: 'In the beginning God created heaven and earth'. But it isn't long before a shepherd is mentioned. In the Bible's fourth chapter we're told that Eve gave birth to Abel, a brother to Cain but a man in a very different mould: 'Abel was a keeper of sheep, but Cain was a tiller of the ground'. And whereas the Lord welcomed Abel's offering of 'the firstlings of the flock and the fat thereof' it seems there was less enthusiasm for Cain's gift of the fruit of the ground (Genesis 4.5).

In Genesis Chapter 29 we read of Jacob, setting forth on his travels, eventually arriving in the land 'of the people of the East'. He spots a well in a field, 'and, lo, there were three flocks of sheep lying by it, for out of that well they watered the flocks; and a great stone was on the well's mouth'.

The special status of pastoral people continues in the New Testament. As the Gospel according to St Luke tells us, in those familiar words, it was a band of shepherds who, 'abiding in the field, keeping watch over their flocks by night', were singled out by the Angel of the Lord to go to Bethlehem and be the first to see 'the babe, wrapped in swaddling clothes and lying in a manger'. And it was those same shepherds who felt that, being the chosen ones, they must go out and broadcast the momentous news of the birth of Jesus.

Why it was that shepherds should be picked to spread the message is difficult to understand. Shepherds, by the very nature of their jobs, tend to be solitary figures who spend much of their lives away from the rest of mankind, with only dogs and sheep as company. Yet the tradition of being a select breed continues to this day. In churches at Christmas it's angels and shepherds who surround the crib as congregations give voice to carols, many of which celebrate the part played by shepherds in the Christmas story:

> *While shepherds watched their flocks by night*
> *All seated on the ground …*

And what self-respecting Nativity play does not include a cluster of tiny children with miniature crooks in hand and heads swathed in towels as they nod approval at the holy infant lying in the manger?

The shepherd as protector of his flock is an image which crops up continuously in the scriptures: 'The Lord is my shepherd; I shall not want ...' (Psalm 23). And the concept of 'good' shepherding can be found in an example of shepherd's lore from the 13th century:

> It profiteth the lord of the manor to have good shepherds, watchful and kindly, so that the sheep be not tormented by their wraths but crop their pasture in peace and joyfulness. For it is the token of the shepherd's kindness if the sheep be not scattered abroad but browse around him in company. Let him provide himself with a good barkable dog and lie nightly with his sheep.

From the Middle Ages onwards two opposing pictures of shepherds were promoted. While the image of the Good Shepherd was still popular in religion, in other forms of literature the shepherd tending his sheep was portrayed as a rustic simpleton. When Queen Elizabeth I visited Sudely Castle in Gloucestershire in 1592 she was greeted, not by a small child with a bouquet but by an address spoken by the lowest of the servants, the shepherd, which began 'Vouchsafe to hear a simple shepherd, because shepherds and simplicity cannot part'.

Such modesty was misplaced, for in the years between 1200 and 1700 wool production boomed in Britain, which would have been impossible without skilled shepherds to oversee the breeding, lambing and shearing of flocks. These men were proud of their calling, not ashamed of it. In fact, so important were they that shepherds were considered to be among the elite of farm labourers. They knew the lore of the countryside.

At the beginning of Queen Victoria's reign in 1837 half the population of the country still worked on the land and the structure of farming was no less feudal than it had been for centuries.

Four-fifths of the country was owned by 7,000 landowners, and 90 per cent of farmers were tenants of those landlords. Agents went between the two groups negotiating rents and programmes of improvement. Recognising that the prosperity of the tenant farmers depended to a large degree on their labourers, landowners set about building cottages to house farm workers and their families. Rows of houses sprang up in farmyards, providing accommodation for stewards, ploughmen, cattlemen, shepherds and 'hinds' – farm servants hired on a six-month or year-long agreement. Round about the 1840s the number of shepherds reached its peak.

What was life like for these men and their families? Well some nineteenth century photographs give the impression that it was idyllic, with flocks grazing quietly in the summer sun watched over by contented shepherds and their faithful dogs. But such pictures were mostly posed, and the reality was very different. While their wives scrimped and saved to feed and clothe their offspring, shepherds spent long hours watching over their sheep. Wages varied from district to district, and from high hill to lowland plain, but by and large, they were low. An article in *The Globe* of July 1878 describes shepherds from the Yorkshire hills gathering at Saltersbrook to celebrate their annual meeting, where 121 stray sheep rounded up on the open moors were returned to their proper flocks. The pay for these men was reckoned to be as little as 17 shillings (about 80p) per week. 'In the summer,' the newspaper reported, 'many of the shepherds sleep out night after night, preferring, when tired and a long distance from their homes, to throw themselves down to rest in the heather.' A 23-year-old shepherd working on Salisbury Plain in 1900 was earning as little as 12 shillings and sixpence (about 62p) a week.

To keep an eye on sheep on Romney Marsh in 1890, a 'looker' received one shilling and sixpence (about 6p) per acre per year. He would have needed contracts for a large number of acres to make a reasonable living.

Badly paid they may have been, but shepherds were expected to give unstintingly of themselves. Writing at the end of the 19th century the farmer and author W.J. Malden made it clear how great those expectations were:

> The shepherd must possess an instinctive love and attachment to animals and must be prepared to sacrifice his personal comfort and ease for the welfare of his flock. In the experience of every shepherd there come times when extraordinary efforts have to be made, entailing strains on his endurance and a demand on his resources. His is a position of great responsibility, and neglect on certain occasions would mean great losses to his employer. Men not accustomed to sheep may walk through them time after time and not recognise ailments until they are very far advanced. A shepherd must be observant, or he is of little value. He must detect the slightest change in his sheep.

Few have shown greater loyalty to their job than the shepherd who tended the flock at Dartmoor Prison in Devon. David Davies was incarcerated in 1879, and knowing he faced a long sentence he applied to look after the prison's sheep, that roamed the nearby moor. For the next 20 years he was trusted to carry out shepherding duties totally unsupervised and it was universally agreed that the sheep were well cared for. At last the time came when he'd served his sentence and was duly released from prison. But he found that life on the outside – without his beloved sheep – was difficult to cope with. Before long he committed another crime and was re-admitted to Dartmoor prison to be reunited with his sheep. This process of release and re-offending continued for a further 30 years until he died in 1929, still a prisoner at Dartmoor – and still keeping watch over his flock. Records of his funeral have not survived, but it wouldn't have been a surprise if his coffin had contained a piece of wool. This was a tradition in many areas. The belief was that on Judgement Day the wool would be proof of the shepherd's vocation, which had prevented him from being a regular attendant at church because he couldn't leave his flock, even on Sundays.

The story of the convict shepherd, however, doesn't end there. It's said that Davies' dedication to his sheep was such that he still returned to his flock … even after he died. But his ghostly grey outline disappears as soon as he is seen by any human; it's for his sheep that he still haunts his old territory.

Shepherds' pay may have been meagre, but sometimes there were hidden extras. In a tradition dating back to the 18th century, some received a portion of their wages in kind. They were allowed to keep a small 'pack' of their master's sheep – anything between five and ten – and they were permitted to sell the lambs and the wool they got from those sheep. Writing in 1900, the author W.H. Hudson lamented the steady decline in the number of shepherds who had 'packs':

It must be a source of regret that the old system of giving a shepherd an interest in the flock was ever changed. In a small way he
was in partnership with his master, the farmer, and regarded
himself, and was regarded by others, as something more than a

mere hireling who looks to receive a few pieces of silver at each week's end and will be no better and no worse off whether the year be fat or lean.

In the North of England and Scotland some farms continue to include a 'pack' in the employment agreement they draw up for their shepherds and some agricultural shows in hill farming areas still have classes for 'pack' sheep, but it is another tradition which is slowly slipping away. 'It's dying out,' says Dave Baxter, one of the hill shepherds featured in this book. 'Not many shepherds have them now. Some had three or four pack sheep, others had a few more. It was a long-standing tradition.' At the annual Blackface ram sales at Lanark in Scotland, many shepherds sell a ram lamb or a shearling ram from their own pack; often they fetch good prices. 'Some of them have a few ewes to breed them from,' Dave says, 'but in the area where I live there aren't many shepherds still doing that.'

Among other ancient customs that endured until the early part of the 20th century was the special system evolved by shepherds to count their sheep. A Sussex farmer writing in 1900 recalled his first job as a shepherd boy on the Downs earning just four pence a day (less than 2p today) back in the middle of the 19th century. He remembered waiting as the old farmer counted sheep by the score (twenty). The boy's job was to remember the number of twenties, but on one occasion he forgot and his master lashed out at him with a chain, cutting him across his forehead. He carried the scar for the rest of his life – and never forgot the Sussex words. They were: *inetherum* (one), *twotherum* (two), *cockerum* (three), *quetherum* (four), *setherum* (five), *shatherum* (six), *wineberry* (seven), *wigtail* (eight), *tarrydiddle* (nine), *den* (ten).

The shepherds in Borrowdale in the Lake District also had a language for counting sheep. But it was very different: *yan, tyan, tethera, methera, pimp, sethera, lethera, hovera, dovera, dick.* The words were like those used by shepherds in other valleys of the Lake District, and there are similarities to sheep-scoring numerals used in Old Welsh, Cornish and Breton. When it came to counting larger flocks shepherds would cut tally sticks from the hedge and carve notches in them for every 20 or 30 sheep that filed by. In some parts of the country they had a number of pebbles in their smocks which they transferred from pocket to pocket as the sheep ran past in groups. But such customs died out long ago.

Putting an exact figure on the number of shepherds remaining in Britain today is not easy. The annual census carried out by the Department for Food and Rural Affairs (Defra) doesn't differentiate between workers whose time is spent exclusively with sheep and those who are employed on mixed farms, but there are clear pointers that shepherd numbers are dropping. For a start, there are only half as many flocks in Britain as there were 50 years ago. Secondly, the migration from rural areas to cities has accelerated. The latest figures available from Defra show that the number of full-time workers on farms in the UK fell from 101,800 in 1996 to 83,800 in 2001, a reduction of 17 per cent. A significant proportion of those must have been shepherds' jobs.

One factor behind the decline is the fall in the value of sheep in real terms. To cover a shepherd's wage and make a reasonable profit, farmers have had to keep more and more sheep. They've also tended to rely more on members of the family to look after their flocks, rather than use hired labour. At the same time there's been a sharp rise in the number of quad bikes on sheep units. They've made the shepherd's (or shepherdess's) job easier, but because they've enabled them to look after bigger flocks they've also contributed to their demise.

1 The Debatable Lands

*M*ost people agree that the logical place to establish an Anglo-Scottish border would have been across the 'neck' of England between Carlisle to Newcastle, the narrowest part of the country and the direction taken by the Roman Wall. But there is nothing logical about this much-disputed frontier, and in fact the border angles north-east from the Solway Firth to Berwick-upon-Tweed rather than running straight across the country. On its way, it passes through the Cheviot Hills, the largest natural barrier between the two nations and the location of some of the wildest and most beautiful country in Britain.

Viewed from Carter Bar, one of the key border crossings, the undulating Cheviots look the picture of innocence, but their soft outlines belie their turbulent history. Roman armies forcibly occupied this land, building roads and forts as they pushed the edge of their empire ever northwards. And for four hundred years between the 13th and the 17th centuries the Cheviots witnessed a relentless cycle of violence as the two neighbouring nations clashed and warlike clans vied for supremacy. Those troubled times have left a legacy: Northumberland, although England's sixth largest county, is still its least densely populated.

It's in the Cheviot foothills that you'll find the two farms where the shepherds interviewed for this book tend their sheep. Dave

Baxter has been shepherd at Linshiels near the village of Alwinton for nearly 40 years, and Stewart and Gwen Wallace are shepherd and shepherdess at Blindburn (the name means 'foaming stream'), ten miles away. Connecting the two places is the Coquet valley, named after the river which splashes its way down from the hills and east across the Northumberland plain before emptying into the North Sea at Amble.

The farms where Dave, Stewart and Gwen are employed date from the late 18th century when prominent landed families in the north-east acquired large tracts of rural Northumberland which they sub-divided and rented out as hill farms. Solid stone farmhouses were built, large enough to accommodate two or three shepherds as well as tenant farmers and their families. In some cases, landowners also added stables with stalls for a cart-horse and a couple of ponies. That they were able to set up farms in this remote area at all was partly due to the peace which settled over the Borders after the abortive Jacobite rebellion in 1715. It's no exaggeration to say that before that there was mayhem. English and Scottish armies were regularly ranged against each other, as at the bloody Battle of Otterburn in 1388, which ended in victory for the Scots, and the Battle of Humbleton Hill, near Wooler, where the English got their revenge 14 years later.

These periodic large-scale military operations ought to have brought stability to the Border area, but they seemed to have had the opposite effect. Mistrust, shifting allegiances and poverty created a society which became a thorn in the side of both the English and the Scottish kings. Far from being a buffer zone between England and Scotland, the Cheviot Hills and the rest of the Borders became a war zone. Bands of men wearing steel bonnets, armed with swords, knives and crude pistols and carrying eight-foot spears 'rode with the moonlight' through the hills. Their steeds were stocky horses familiar with traversing secret tracks through valleys and over moors, and their purpose was the indiscriminate plundering of sheep, cattle and horses from neighbours' land across the border. Anyone who stood in their way was brutally murdered.

It's tempting to lay the blame on one side or the other. The bitter feelings of Northumbrians who were victims of Scottish aggression are summed up in lines written at the time:

> *God send the land deliverance*
> *Frae every reiving, riding Scot*
> *We'll sune hae neither cow nor ewe*
> *We'll sune hae neither stag nor stot*

But the truth is that Scottish and English were equally guilty. Records show that between 1510 and 1603 armed gangs made 1,145 separate raids across the Border and that they came from each side in equal number. A state of anarchy prevailed and The Borders became known, rightly, as 'The Debateable Lands'.

In this dangerous environment one option was to join one of the delinquent families and hope that they would provide protection from retaliatory attacks. Among the clans on the Northumberland side were the much-feared Charltons, Dodds, Robsons and Milburns, who launched their forays into Scotland from Tynedale, and the Hills, Dunns, Hedleys and Reeds who were based in Redesdale. But as well as staging hit-and-run raids across the Border, families fought among themselves. One contemporary historian wrote:

The people of this country hath had one barbarous custome amongst them. If any two be displeased they expect no lawe but bang it out bravely, one and his kindred against another and his; they will subject themselves to no justice, but in an inhumane and barbarous manner fight and kill one another. They run together in clangs [clans] as thy terme it. This fighting they call 'feides' [feuds].

As the notoriety of the area spread, both Scottish and English kings appointed wardens to control the nefarious activities of the 'Border Reivers'. But these purported peace-keepers proved to be almost as duplicitous as the thieves themselves, turning a blind eye to their lawless behaviour in return for a share of the spoils.

Poorer families, who lived in hovels made from wood, clay, turf and stones, still tried to rear their own animals and grow crops of oats, rye and barley, but theirs was a life full of uncertainty. The more well-off constructed simple but effective tower houses out of stone hewn from local quarries or salvaged from buildings laid waste by the reivers. Called 'pele' towers, they were often ringed by a stockade behind which livestock and horses could take shelter. In a survey compiled in 1415 more than 100 such castles and 'fortalices' (fortresses) are listed in Northumberland alone, so one could expect to find a similar number on the Scottish side of the frontier.

How did the general sense of insecurity affect the majority of the people who lived through the troubled times? It made them self-sufficient, but wary – traits which in many ways they retain to this day. In 1599 the historian William Camden visited Redesdale and Coquetdale and reported that 'In the wasts, as they terme them, you may see the ancient nomads, a martiall kinde of men, who from the month of April unto August lye out scattering and summering with their cattell in little cottages which they call shielings.' Camden was too frightened to venture into a part of west Northumberland, closer to the border, because he had heard that the 'moss troopers' still resided there.

While calm may have descended on the border lands in the 18th century, illegal activities continued in the Cheviot Hills including smuggling and the unlicensed brewing of liquor. In *Highways and Byways of Northumbria*, written at the beginning of the 20th century, the local historian Anderson Graham recounts a visit to a waterfall on the Usway burn, close to which were the well-preserved remains of a still which belonged to Rory, a noted distiller of 'mountain dew' – as it was euphemistically dubbed. Not far from there as the crow flies, at Rowhope burn mouth, stood an inn which rejoiced in the evocative name of 'Slyme Foot'. There, in the 18th century, the farmers of the district 'spent much of their time gambling and drinking illicit whisky, which came from numerous distilleries among the hills'. So popular was the peat-flavoured spirit that there were even some 'gaugers', the excisemen who were supposed to arrest the distillers, who were happy to let the practice continue, having themselves – it's said – become semi-addicted to the brew.

By the beginning of the 19th century farming in the Cheviots had settled into a more regular pattern and was relatively prosperous, judging by documents recently acquired by Beamish Museum in County Durham. They are handbills made by a printer from Alnwick in Northumberland, most of them advertising auction sales held on farms 200 years ago. A typical example announces a 'large' sale to be held at The Heigh, a farm at Alwinton, near Rothbury on Monday, 14th May, 1832, on behalf of Robert Wetherson who is 'leaving this country'. The livestock on offer was 'all the shepherd's stock' consisting of 42 ewes with their recently-born lambs, 45 gimmers and dinmonts (once-sheared sheep, female and male), 40 ewe and wedder hoggs (the previous year's lambs, both sexes), and three cows. Farm equipment included a single-horse cart with assorted bits of harness, a ladder, rakes, forks, grapes and scythes. Among the pieces of household furniture were three 'excellent close and other beds', a large kitchen press and chest, a dresser and shelves, an eight-day clock, large 'wainscot, kitchen and tea' tables and four chairs. 'The above furniture is nearly new and in excellent condition,' the bill states. Also being sold by the auctioneer, William Donkin, of Rothbury, were dairy utensils consisting of a cheese press, barrel churn, skeels (scales), tubs, bowls 'and every other appendage'.

The date of the sale – 14th May – is interesting. Rented farms usually change hands at May Term, 13th May, but that was a Sunday in 1832, which explains why the sale was delayed for 24 hours. Another point of interest is the reason for the sale – that the tenant farmer was 'leaving this country'. My guess is that he was moving to another farm away from the Alwinton area ('this country') and not that he was emigrating. As for referring to the sheep and cows as the 'shepherd's stock', the advert must mean the stock looked after (but, of course, not owned) by the shepherd. Robert Wetherson was a farmer, and a reasonably prosperous one at that. With his eight-day clock and cheese-making equipment, he was probably an upwardly-mobile young man with his eye on a bigger and better farm.

Meanwhile, it's ironic that the Cheviot Hills, which were riven by dispute and then restored to tranquillity, should once again become the scene of military activities. But that has been their fate. Since the early years of the 20th century most of the farms in the upper Coquet valley, along with many others in this corner of Northumberland, have been owned by the Ministry of Defence and are part of the Otterburn Training Ranges. There are no steel bonnets in sight, and mortars have replaced muskets. But the warlike nature of the area is not entirely forgotten, especially when the guns start their distant rumbling.

2 Lamb's Tales

Sheep are believed to have been the second wild animals to have been domesticated by man, after he'd tamed wild dogs and got them to work for him. No one is sure when that happened, but evidence suggests that it was some time around 10,000 BC. Since then, sheep have been bred for a wide range of characteristics. Versatile herbivores, they are kept for their fibre, pelts, milk and meat and have the useful knack of being able to exploit land which cannot be cultivated for crops.

Primitive sheep still exist in some parts of the world, including the mouflon of Europe and Asia Minor, the urial of western Asia (probably the first sheep bred in captivity) and the argali of Central Asia. But the 200 breeds which cover the globe today are very different from those early types. Nowadays, many sheep are the result of two breeds being crossed to produce an animal that makes the most of local growing conditions.

Sheep had a major influence on the spread of civilization. Tribes living on the plains of Mesopotamia, where the average temperature was a moderate 70°F, were able to expand into harsher climates once they had discovered the advantages of wool clothing. Not only that, they could also take their food supply along with them, in the shape of their flocks.

The way sheep have been looked after has been surprisingly consistent across cultures. One of the earliest methods of farming in the hills is known as 'transhumance', which involved nomadic herdsmen driving cattle, sheep and goats from lowland pastures to land in the hills once the snows melted. Sheep were usually watched over by men with guard dogs or were trained to follow a 'leader' sheep as they journeyed towards their summer grazings. In the autumn they travelled back down to the lowlands. In some countries this seasonal migration continues to this day.

It's received wisdom that the industries which put the 'great' into Great Britain were coal, steel, shipbuilding and manufactured goods. And in the eighteenth and nineteenth centuries that was certainly the case. But in the hundreds of years before the industrial revolution the main source of Britain's wealth was wool.

The Romans are understood to have been the first to recognise the potential of Britain for wool production and it was they who established large-scale sheep farming here. They are credited with the development of long-woolled, white-faced sheep in the lowland areas of Britain and types with coarser and shorter wool in the uplands. They also set up woolly processing centres in places like Winchester in Hampshire.

England was well established as a trader in wool by the time of the Norman invasion and wool production was an industry that went on to grow dramatically through medieval times. 'Baa Baa Black Sheep' is said to be the oldest nursery rhyme on record. It dates from 1275 and refers to bags of wool being counted for export tax.

Over the centuries farmers have striven to breed sheep to suit the circumstances of their farms, and the early 1800s saw the development of the New Leicester and Southdown breeds which became the basis of today's lowland sheep. One of the first breeds to make an impression in mountainous regions was the Blackface. It's difficult to pinpoint when the breed first emerged as a distinctive type, but there are records from monasteries in the 12th century which refer to the 'dun or blackface' breed of sheep. Monks used the wool for their clothes and exported large amounts to Europe.

In the 16th century King James IV of Scotland established an improved Blackface flock in the Ettrick Forest in Selkirkshire. During the 17th and 18th centuries these animals were known as 'Linton sheep', West Linton in Peebleshire being the main sale venue for animals of this type. In the early 19th century Blackface sheep were taken from Dumfriesshire and Lanarkshire and introduced into the North of Scotland but, due to the high price of Cheviot wool, Blackfaces were cleared off the hills in favour of the Cheviot. This continued until 1860 when the wool prices reached the same level and many farmers realised that, with its ability to survive and reproduce in adverse weather conditions, the Blackface was just as well suited to utilise hill and mountain grazing as the Cheviot. Today the Blackface breed is the most numerous in Britain, amounting to more than three million ewes and representing 16 per cent of the British pure-bred ewe flock.

Blackfaces are horned sheep with black or black and white face and legs. The fleece varies from short, fine wool used in carpets and tweeds to strong, coarse wool used in mattresses. There are three types: the Perth type, the Lanark type and the large-framed, soft-woolled Northumberland type. The main purpose of the breed is to produce store lambs which are suitable for fattening off grass, rape, turnips or fodder. On better hill grazings many lambs grow quickly and are fat enough to be sold to butchers straight off their mothers. Its proponents assert that the meat has an unrivalled sweet flavour and tenderness.

Blackfaces are also part of the pyramid of stratification of the British sheep-breeding industry. Drafted off the hills as five- or six-year-old ewes they are crossed with Bluefaced Leicesters to produce Mule ewes or with Border Leicesters to produce Greyface ewes. These in turn are crossed with terminal sires such as Suffolks or Texels to produce fat lambs.

Pictures of Blackface rams bought at Lanark a hundred years ago show animals with speckled faces and legs and long fleeces. In wintry conditions, the fleeces used to ball up with snow as they dragged along the ground. Over the years, breeders introduced some Swaledale blood into the Blackfaces to shorten the length of their coats, improve their mothering ability and give them longer legs.

Since the hills of the Scottish Borders began to be stocked with sheep, it wasn't just the Blackface breed which dominated. As I mentioned earlier, Cheviots were favoured by many farmers. The breed is first referred to in 1372 as 'a small but very hardy race' found over large tracts of the Cheviot Hills. Hardy it would certainly need to be: the area at the time was being continuously laid to waste by the Border Reivers and sheep, along with other livestock, were regarded as fair game.

3 Dave Baxter

$\mathcal{A}$t 5 p.m. on January 15th, 1959, a new regional broadcaster, Tyne Tees Television, began transmitting programmes in the north-wast of England. One of the first programmes the company developed was *Farming Outlook* and for almost three decades it went out at lunchtime on Sunday, giving viewers a well-researched window on rural life. With its mixture of topical studio discussions and filmed reports, it built up a loyal following. I produced the programme in the late 1980s. As well as covering serious issues we were always looking for light-hearted topics and one summer an opportunity presented itself which we thought might bring a smile to the faces of viewers.

At that time quad bikes were beginning to make an impact on farms in Britain, and to assess their real value – and have some fun – Hexham Young Farmers' Club in Northumberland came up with the idea of staging a 'One Man and his Bike' competition. At Highwood Farm on the outskirts of Hexham they constructed an obstacle course consisting of several pairs of gates and invited contestants on bikes to try to drive a small group of sheep through them. Needless to say, there were some chaotic attempts to complete the course. But it did produce a champion, the local farmer David Nixon.

On *Farming Outlook*, we thought we'd take this tongue-in-cheek test a stage further by pitting David and his quad bike against a leading shepherd and his dog to see which method – ancient or modern – would be best for herding sheep. The shepherd we invited was Dave Baxter. Dave was one of Northumberland's leading sheepdog handlers at the time and I asked him if he would like to take part in our unusual competition. Never being one to walk away from a challenge, however daft, he said yes. We decided to use the existing course at Highwood Farm as the location for our quad-v-dog comparison, with Jim Easton, another well-known dog handler, as judge.

For the record, the surprising victor in our contest was David Nixon and his bike. For some reason the four sheep he was given were happy to be shunted round the obstacle course by a man on a quad, whereas the presence of Dave Baxter and his dog seemed to unsettle them. 'They were jumpy,' Dave recalls. 'They were't used to being herded with a dog.'

Whatever the competition, Dave wants to come first. So, to be beaten – and by a bloke on a bike at that – did rankle a little. Not that he showed it, of course. He insists that he enjoyed the day. 'It was just a bit of fun,' he says. 'It was an interesting experience. I've done some unusual things in my time, like doing an exhibition of herding geese with a sheepdog. But that day was a bit different.'

Farming is in Dave's blood. He was born on 31st August, 1938, at Plantation Farm between Chatton and Belford in north Northumberland. He has two brothers and a sister, and when he was three the family moved to a nearby farm called South Hazelrigg. It was typical of the large farms of the area with 1,000 acres of what's known as 'in-bye' (lowland cropping ground) and 500 acres of hill. Two rows of farm workers' cottages lined the road approaching the farm and even then, two years into the Second World War, there were still ten men and their families living on the holding.

Dave's father David was one of the last of a breed of men who were regarded with awe in agriculture: the horsemen. These hired workers had a special way with the giant Clydesdales they tamed and worked with; they understood the horses, and the horses would do anything for them. On farms such as South Hazelrigg the horsemen's working lives were governed by strict discipline and a strong sense of order. They were expected to rise at 5.30 in the morning to go and feed their horses, then grab a hasty break- fast before harnessing up in readiness for the day's work. At seven, they would prepare to leave the stables.

Dave's father's position was 'ploughman steward'. In other words, he was the head horseman, the man who decided how the fields should be ploughed – and who set the standard for good ploughing. In arable farming areas of Britain, this had been the pattern for more than a century. There was a strict hierarchy among the labour force and it was customary for the head horse- man to be the first to leave the farmyard and set off for the day's work. Everyone else took their cue from him. At noon, when he stopped for his 'bait' (snack) and 'lowsed' (loosed) out his horses, the rest of the horsemen stopped and loosed out theirs too. And when the day was done and it was time to return to the farm, it was the head horsemen who led the way. 'I was just a tot,' Dave says, 'but I can remember it well, that feeling of pride seeing my father driving the first pair of horses.'

The steady pace of life on the land, so enjoyed by many in the first half of the 20th century, started to hasten as the years rolled by. At South Hazelrigg the turning point came in 1949. The owner of the farm called in at Hendersons, the agricultural engineers in Kelso, Roxburghshire, and bought his first tractor. It was only a little Ferguson, but its purchase was symbolic – it was the beginning of the end for the horses.

Dave's grandfather on his mother's side had been a shepherd and, keen though he was on heavy horses, Dave found himself becoming more and more fascinated by sheep. His grandfather had been a useful dog handler and he encouraged Dave to take an interest in Border Collies, with the result that at the age of 12 Dave got his first sheepdog, Don. Prior to that he'd knocked about with an old farm dog called Glen. 'I got him from an old shepherd called Willie Buchanan. He was one of the characters of the hills. I used to help him at lambing time as a boy and he let me have a pup in return. I thought he was the best dog there'd ever been. I trained him in my own tinpot style, and at the time I reckoned I'd done a magnificent job on him. Of course, when I look back, I hadn't. But to me – just starting out – Don was great.'

Soon after he left the tiny school in the hamlet of Hazelrigg at the age of 15, Dave spotted an advert in the local paper: 'Shepherd Lad Required'. It was what he'd dreamed of, so he was delighted when he was taken on for the job. He was on the first rung of the ladder. 'In those days, farms used to take on apprentice shepherds, which sadly they no longer do. It was a good system because it kept the supply of shepherds going. But now that it's stopped, there are very few young people coming into the game. That's why it's a dying trade.'

In 2003 two Northumberland-born authors published a light-hearted book dedicated to the apprentices who were taken on by farmers at the same time that Dave Baxter was starting. Called *Daft Laddies* it's the work of former university lecturer Clive

Dalton, who hails from Bellingham but now lives in New Zealand, and Donald Clegg, an ex-teacher who lives in the village of Falstone in the heart of the Kielder Forest. Both writers had spells as 'farm laddies' in their youth in the North Tyne valley and they still smile grimly when they recall the way they were treated, both by the men they worked for and by the regular farm workers. All of them had come up the hard way and no allowances were made for the fact that the lads were still wet behind the ears.

'We were the new recruits', Don remembers. 'We knew nothing. If we ever had an idea or an opinion, it was guaranteed to be considered daft by the old hands on the farm. No brains and big gobs were our permanent afflictions! But we learned a lot, not just about the skills required to be a farm worker. We also learned much about animal and human behaviour.'

On the small valley farms where they served their time, Clive Dalton and Don Clegg remember that there was always a farm dog, semi-retired and stiff in the joints but still with a mind of its own. 'As the farm laddie you weren't expected to own a dog. But you were certainly expected to use the farm dog for everyday chores like getting the cows in for milking, bringing the outlying cattle up for their hay or shifting the ewes on a summer's evening before you went home.

'There was generally no problem. Most times the dog totally ignored your directions as it knew these jobs far better than you did. But there was a real frustration in emergencies, such as the time the cows did a merry dance in the ripening barley while the boss was away at the auction mart. This was when you desperately needed a dog. But nothing would get the old farm dog out of its house, not even the missus with a bit of the butcher's best spare rib. You could try all the nice dog noises you could think of, but all you got in response was the sound of the tail wagging on the wooden floor!'

Of course, Dave Baxter, with his passion for dogs, had a head start. When he started in his first job he already had his own Border Collie and didn't need to whistle up the old farm dog. He was confident in his own ability.

The farm where Dave began his career was Sourhope, a 2,640 acre (1,100 hectare) sheep unit situated in the picturesque valley of Bowmont Water, on the Scottish side of the Cheviot Hills. It was run by the newly-launched Hill Farming Research Organisation, which carried out trials into crops, sheep grazing regimes, land fertility and many other subjects. Pronounced 'Soor-up', the farm, rented from Roxburgh Estates, is still an experimental hill farming unit, but today it comes under the wing of the Macaulay Land Use Research Institute.

Three full-time shepherds were employed on the farm, one single and two married. Dave had lodgings with one of the married shepherds. 'It was a good arrangement,' he says. 'They got paid for feeding you, and you were well looked after.'

For the young shepherd, lodging in a shepherd's cottage and earning just a few pounds, it was a hard baptism: 'You were up with the lark every morning. You learned how to run dogs, how to handle sheep properly and how to shear by hand. There was a lot to it.' As shepherd laddie, he had his own small hill and his own small flock of sheep to tend, mirroring the senior shepherds on the farm as, in time-honoured fashion, they 'raked' (drove) their sheep down the hill in the morning and back up the hill at night.

'You were overseen by an older man. He kept you right, told you what to do and what not to do. If you were clever enough to listen to the old shepherds you got on well. But if you thought you knew it all, you didn't last long. It was seven days a week, and you had to stick at it. But there was give-and-take. If you wanted a day off you could have it, so long as you were there when the work was to be done at lambing time or clipping time. People weren't in such a hurry in those days. There were more men to tend the farms and every hill had a shepherd on it; now there's one shepherd to three of four hills. It's just the way it's changed. One man's doing three men's work.'

The direction Sourhope has taken has also changed. Britain's 'Dig-For-Victory' efforts during the Second World War, when subsidy payments helped food production to soar by 50 per cent, were hailed as an outstanding achievement. While Dave was learning his trade on Sourhope's broad acres, the farming industry, encouraged by the Government, was still worshipping at the altar of increased output. For the last few years, however, the emphasis has been very different. Policy makers, anxious to preserve moorland birds, wild flowers and rare grasses, want hill farmers to keep fewer sheep and, where possible, they'd like them to diversify. As someone who spent his formative years shepherding sheep at Sourhope, Dave would be surprised to learn that it's now home to the country's largest cashmere-goat herd.

Moreover, the farm has been the scene of an unusual experiment. The oddly-named 'thoka' gene for fecundity, which originally occurred in Icelandic sheep, was introduced to the UK in 1985 in a bid to make some of our sheep breeds more fertile. Through a programme of cross breeding conducted by the Macaulay Institute the gene was established in Cheviot sheep, a breed which doesn't normally produce more than one lamb a year. Cheviot ewes at Sourhope are now retained as 'thoka carriers' – but only if they have lambed in each of their first three years and had at least two sets of twins. The implications of these trials are far-reaching. Despite being forced to keep fewer sheep, hill flocks consisting of Thoka Cheviots may be able to maintain the number of lambs they produce because the ewes are more prolific.

This was in Sourhope's future, but Dave Baxter, as he honed his skills as a shepherd, found he was getting restless. He left Sourhope to 'work loose': lambing a lowland flock in March at one farm, a hill flock in April at another, and shearing sheep in the summer. The casual work was readily available, but then he fancied being in full-time employment again. He'd bought a motorbike and needed money for petrol. This time, the post wasn't advertised. Dave heard about it on the bush telegraph.

Uswayford Farm, on the Northumberland side of the Border high in the Cheviots, is where Dave got his next permanent job. Back in the 1930s the farm had featured in the *Newcastle Journal* in an article by a writer called Paul Brown, entitled 'Uswayford – The Lonely Farm'. Uswayford (pronounced locally as 'Yoozey Ford') is reached by taking the winding road up the Coquet valley and then forking off towards the North. It's a distance of some ten miles from the village of Alwinton, and they seem to be very long miles indeed. On the occasion of Paul Brown's visit, the farm was cut off by snow but the intrepid scribe wasn't put off. He made his way there by horse and cart.

When Dave arrived at Uswayford in 1958 it was certainly as remote as Brown makes out, but nowhere near as lonely. There were three shepherds looking after the sheep on the extensive hill farm. Two were single and one had a family. 'It was good fun,' Dave recalls. 'There were lots of us. We had plenty of entertain-ment.' Fifty years ago, people's existence on remote farms like

Uswayford was, in many ways, the same as it had been since the 19th century. Cut off from the rest of the world, with just a horse or a pony as transport, families had to be self-sufficient. Hens laid eggs, a house cow supplied milk both to drink and make butter from, bacon and ham came from the pig that was fattened and slaughtered every year, and there was mutton from the occasional home-killed sheep. A row or two of potatoes were planted in a field close to the farm and a well-stocked garden grew vegetables, fruit and an assortment of flowers.

The dominant feature of farmhouse kitchens was the huge black range with its glowing grate, heavy oven door and gleaming brass fender. In those days, the hearth was the centre of the home and polishing the range was a daily ritual. The fire boiled pans, heated the oven, warmed the house and consumed much of the rubbish. As hot water was constantly needed, the kettle was never far from boiling. Suspended over the flames, like a blackened gallows, was a metal arm. From it usually hung a cauldron containing concoctions such as vegetable broth, mutton stew or blackcurrant jam, and the room would always be redolent with the smell of cooking.

The kitchen's layout might vary from farm to farm, but many of the contents would be the same : the cured hams hanging from hooks in the ceiling, the seasoning hazel sticks (to be made into crooks) slotted between beams, the strips of sticky brown fly-paper, the stone-flagged floor and the colourful "clippie" mats made on winter nights from scraps of discarded material. Since there was no electricity, rooms had to be illuminated by paraffin lamps and candles.

Upstairs, every bed had a chamber pot lurking beneath it, as visiting the "netty" (toilet) was not something to be attempted at night since it involved a journey of some distance to a dry closet at the bottom of the garden. Few farms had bathrooms. Instead, families washed in the scullery or bathed in a long tin bath in front of the fire. By today's standards it was spartan, especially when the winter nights set in, the draughts blew under the doors and frost left intricate patterns on the windows. But at the time it seemed cosy to the inhabitants of those isolated settlements.

At Uswayford, Dave was allocated a hill to shepherd. It stretched right out to the top of The Cheviot, a height of 2,676 feet (815 metres) and was covered in places with 'moss haggs', tall clumps of peat which made it difficult to even see the sheep, never mind gather them. 'It was different then,' he says. 'You didn't ride around on a bike. If you were going to the hill, you had to walk there and walk back. It was a hell of a distance.'

As on lowland farms, there was something of a hierarchy on the 3,800-acre unit. The place was run by the head shepherd, Dawson Telfer, and he and his wife had five children. The youngest was Mona, and after a while she and Dave started courting. They were married in 1961 in the beautiful St Michael's Church in Alwinton, just a few hundred yards away from where they now live. But the location for the reception was, typically, up in the hills – the isolated village hall at Windyhaugh.

After they married, Dave moved farms, this time to work for the Carruthers family, first at Whiskershiel, near Elsdon, and then at Linshiels, 3,000 acres of heathery moor just outside Alwinton. 'There were two of us to begin with,' Dave says. 'Then the other man left and I did it myself after that. I must have walked thousands of miles over that farm. In almost 40 years on one place you get to know every inch of it, all the sheep tracks, all the paths, all the places where sheep conceal themselves when you're out with the dogs trying to gather them. You can see most of the farm when you get out on the tops, and that's an advantage.'

People wonder how shepherds stick at their jobs, far removed from the rest of civilisation and with only their dogs as company. 'It's never bothered me,' Dave says. 'I liked it that way. I've worked in isolated places all my life.' Being filmed for a documentary series can be an exposing experience, I would be the first to admit. But Dave, who is in many ways a private person, took to it with enthusiasm, answering questions straightforwardly, relating interesting stories from his life, and often anticipating the kind of activities we might like to film. Working alone, as he says, hadn't affected him that much. The only time the remoteness of the job really came home to him was late one summer afternoon more than 15 years ago. 'I was standing on a rock at the top of Barrow Hill, whistling my dogs, when the rock suddenly gave way under me. There was a sharp pain and I knew at once I'd broken my leg.' He was stranded on an 800-foot summit almost two miles from home, and there was only one way to get back – crawl. At least, like all good shepherds, he had a stick to take his weight as he struggled through the heather. Several hours later he was rescued by his son Bruce who, worried when his father didn't return at the usual time, had set off on a tractor to look for him. 'It wasn't something I would like to go through again,' Dave says, 'but I've been lucky on the whole. That was the only real injury I've had.'

Shepherds' families raised on remote farms learn from neces-sity to be self-sufficient and Dave and Mona are no exception. As recently as 1988, long after most farms had given up keeping a house cow, they were still milking theirs and Mona was making butter from her milk. The cow was a Shorthorn, a breed much loved by shepherds but which even then was becoming scarce.

Keeping your own cow might seem strange to those whose milk comes in a carton from the supermarket, but in the country habits of a lifetime are hard to shake off.

The following words, often spoken as grace at a country dinner, capture the life that Dave, and shepherds like him, has enjoyed:

> *The wealthy and great*
> *May roll in their state*
> *I envy them not I declare it*
> *I eat my own lamb*
> *My chicken and ham*
> *I shear my own fleece*
> *And I wear it.*

Dave and Mona live in a shepherd's house called 'Angryhaugh' (the name means 'flat grazing land by the river'). A productive garden – Dave excels at growing dahlias – surrounds the house. They have their flock of hens, as a few people still do on outlying places. They're an old breed, Brown Leghorn, and their plumage is beautiful; Dave rears chicks in an incubator, so he has a continuous supply of new hens.

Visitors to Angryhaugh are invariably given a warm welcome and plied with cups of tea and platefuls of home-made scones. Mona is a generous and kind woman, interested in other people but preferring to stay well out of the limelight herself. If we were filming in her proximity she'd say fiercely: 'Don't point that camera at me. You don't want me in your film!' As well as Bruce, Dave and Mona have a daughter, Caroline, and another son, David. Despite their father's love of the land, they have all chosen different paths and none of them are in farming.

On August 31st 2003, his 65th birthday, Dave retired from his job as shepherd at Linshiels. Looking back on his life, he says: 'I've been happy shepherding. I've had a lot of good times. It's what I wanted to do – and it's what I did.'

4 Gwen Wallace

*E*very September for almost 40 years a small group of students has assembled at Kirkley Hall, Northumberland's agricultural college, at the start of a new academic year. Standing under the magnificent cedar tree that has graced the hall's courtyard for almost two centuries, they listen to the speeches of welcome from lecturers as they wait to be shown round the college. In most respects they look like any other bunch of students on their first day at college, some nervous, some confident. But one thing is different. Each student is holding a Border Collie dog on a lead. That's because these college beginners are about to embark on a unique course: they're all going to train to be shepherds.

Since this unusual course was launched in 1965 more than 500 shepherds – male and female – have been trained at Kirkley Hall. The majority have been from Britain, but over the years the college has also recruited students from New Zealand, Australia, Japan, North America, the Nordic countries and Europe. All of them have taken an Advanced National Certificate in Agriculture (ANCA) course in sheep management. It's special for a number of reasons. Other colleges may run courses in how to look after lowland sheep, but Kirkley Hall is the only one in the country which offers tuition in hill sheep management as well. And to make sure they turn out to be all-round shepherds, they're also taught how to train and work their sheepdogs.

Many other components, theoretical and practical, go into making the 37-week course different. But it was the chance to learn about both hill and lowland sheep farming systems which made Gwen Roberts put her name forward for the shepherds' course in the summer of 1986. In short, it was everything she was looking for.

Gwen is a warm, friendly individual with a winning smile. She has a wicked sense of humour and likes to give people a gentle ribbing, especially when they're a rather serious-minded television producer like myself. Asked if she'd mind if we filmed her working as a shepherdess, her response was immediate: 'Not at all. When do you want to start?' I knew immediately it was intended as an offer of help, and not in any way as a promotion of herself.

Diminutive and energetic, Gwen would describe herself as mad about animals. She certainly developed her interest in farming when she was very young. 'I was born in Bangor, North Wales, but when I was growing up we lived on the Isle of Anglesey. My father worked at a chemical factory, nothing to do with agriculture at all, but my mother comes from Lancashire and she was brought up on a farm so I think farming may be in the blood.

'I went to the local primary school in Llangristiolus. The people in the village wanted somebody to look after the chapel, and the house went with the job so we moved in. We had a rent-free house, with my mother cleaning the chapel, and my father still had full-time work. Nearby there was a farm run by two bachelor brothers and my mother did some housekeeping for them, two or three days a week. I've got two sisters and when we were off school we'd go with our mother and help out on the farm. It was a sheep and beef farm, one of the largest on Anglesey, and we used to love going when it was lambing time. At other times of the year we'd help with feeding the animals and dipping the sheep. We just used to follow the farmers around, helping out. I used to cycle there and spend Saturday at the farm. I was so interested in the animals I used to be waiting for the farmers – wishing they would hurry up – when they came out of the house to start the day's work!'

Gwen left school when she was 16 and went to an agricultural college in Llangefni on Anglesey. 'I did a Youth Training Scheme. I went to college two or three days a week and the rest of the time I worked on a farm just down the road, travelling there on my moped. I did that for a year. The YTS worked quite well for the farmer, because he only had to pay you about £10 a week, but at the same time you gained a lot of experience.'

As time went by it became clearer to Gwen that she wanted to specialise in one aspect of farming. 'I really wanted to work with sheep,' she says. 'So I set about finding out which college might suit me the best. A college down south, Hampshire I think it was, did a course in lowland sheep management, but the Northumberland college at Kirkley Hall was the only place in Britain where you could do a course in both hill and lowland sheep. I was 18 then but when I went for an interview at the college they said I was too young. They wanted me to have another year's experience, working with sheep.

'It was a bit of a setback, but I was very lucky in that I got a job working for a man called Lord Stanley. He was a very good boss. It was a lowland farm and I worked there for a year, which was really good. I was offered a job there at the end of the year, but I turned it down. I'd set my mind on doing the sheep course and it's the best thing I ever did.'

Kirkley Hall, which is situated near Ponteland on the northern outskirts of Newcastle-upon-Tyne, is a fine stone building dating back to 1764. The college has its own lowland farm with an 18th-century, red brick farmhouse, and it rents a hill farm called Carlcroft, which borders Blindburn at the head of the Coquet valley in Northumberland. In some years, the number of students on the shepherds' course has been as high as 22. When Gwen began the course in 1987 there was a healthy intake of 14 including four women. 'I really enjoyed that year at college,' Gwen says. 'Most of us were aged about 19 but there was one woman in her thirties. We all got on well and I'm still in contact with some of them. I was really pleased I did the course.'

Not only are rooms provided for students, but their dogs, an essential part of the course, are given accommodation too, in kennels. 'It was really interesting because you had to bring a dog to the college to train, something between ten and fifteen months old,' says Gwen. 'I'd always liked dogs and in particular sheepdogs. The interest was definitely always there, right from the beginning. My first Border Collie was called Mot. I can't remember how old I was, but I'd be just a teenager, still living at home. He was just a pet, but I think he would have worked sheep, given the chance. He had the ability.

'When I knew I was going to Kirkley Hall I got a sheepdog called Taff from a bloke on Anglesey who ran dogs at sheepdog trials and who had some pups at the time. Taff was about six or seven weeks old when I got him. I remember going into this old farm building and picking him up and then realising that between his paws he had lots of ticks, the poor little thing! It was horrible. But those kind of things do happen and I got him sorted out. He turned out fine.

'I didn't really do any sheep work with him before I went to the college because I had to get to work on the moped, and there's no room for a dog on a moped! By the time I took him up to Northumberland he was about a year old, and still untrained. The shepherd at Kirkley Hall, Ron Bailey, was a good dog handler and a nice man, very straight and to the point. We would have a lesson with him once a week and he would tell us what to do. I didn't know how to train a dog, but he taught you. He would take you and your dog into a small field with some sheep and he'd see how the dog did, and he would tell you what you should do and shouldn't do.'

Remembering how enthusiastic Taff was, Gwen laughs. 'Taff was a very keen dog, sometimes too keen. But he was a natural, which helped a lot, and I won the prize for being the most improved dog handler at the college with him. It's the luck of the draw, choosing a pup. After you've had some practice you start to know what you're looking for, but it doesn't always work out the way you thought it would. There was one student in our group who had a dog that wasn't really interested in sheep, and it was a problem for her.'

One of the most useful parts of the shepherds' course is the practical experience gained at lambing time. In March, students have to spend three weeks lambing ewes on a lowland farm in Northumberland or the eastern Borders of Scotland, followed by three weeks in April helping with the lambing on a hill farm. There has never been any problem finding placements for the students at lambing time. Farmers recognise that they've been well trained and are happy to take them on as paid assistants.

Gwen remembers this part of the course as being a bit of a breakthrough for her. 'For my hill lambing I went to a farm,

Ewartley Shank, near Alnham in the Cheviot Hills. I was really nervous because I'd never worked on a hill before, but they were nice people and I was able to run my dog for the first time. I enjoyed the three weeks so much.' There was another plus: the farmer's wife was an excellent cook. 'The food was fantastic,' laughs Gwen. 'I didn't really want to leave!'

The other enjoyable part of the sheep management course was being taught the right way to shear. With some experience of clipping days on farms where she'd worked before going to college, Gwen wasn't a complete novice. But her technique improved dramatically at Kirkley Hall. 'The tuition for shearing was excellent. I got the bronze and the silver seal from the British Wool Marketing Board. To qualify, you had to clip so many in a certain time – and do it right. And as a group we used to go to different farms to clip. The college allowed students to do that. The farmers got their sheep clipped for nothing, and it was good experience for us. I found with clipping that it's just a question of getting the right technique. I'm not fast but I'm tidy. I prefer to catch the sheep myself, because it's a chance to stretch and go and get your sheep, whereas if there's someone catching the sheep there's no chance to have a break. But aside from that, I like clipping.'

Since June 1988, when Gwen left Kirkley Hall at the end of her spell at the college, the shepherds' course has continued to attract students. But two factors have caused numbers to fall in recent times: declining incomes on sheep units, which have forced farmers to cut back on staff, and foot and mouth disease, which brought about the slaughter of four and a half million sheep in 2001.

In the September of that year Kirkley Hall had been about to start yet another sheep management course when, in an attempt to halt the further spread of foot and mouth, Defra imposed an order banning the movement of livestock over a vast expanse of south Northumberland. Eight of the ten students who had signed up for the new course were based outside the county. Understandably, they were reluctant to attend a college in an area affected by such wide-ranging restrictions, and so the shepherds' course was cancelled. The following year, with sheep farming still recovering from the impact of the epidemic, the course was scrapped again.

Now part of Northumberland College, Kirkley Hall re-launched the course in September 2003. In its new guise it includes all the previous components, together with some new options, among them instruction on using all-terrain vehicles. In 2003/4 seven students were signed up and, while that's nowhere near the numbers of the course's heyday, it's hoped that the uptake will increase. The reputation of Kirkley Hall stands students in good stead and, up to now, they've invariably found work once they have completed the course. The only cloud on the horizon has been a trend for farmers to rely more and more on family members to look after their sheep during most of the year, and call in contractors at busy periods.

Gwen didn't land a job straight away when she left Kirkley Hall. 'My intention was to go back to Wales, but I couldn't find work. Then I remembered seeing an advert for this job at Blindburn pinned up on a noticeboard at college, and I went and had an interview and was really pleased when I got it.'

She vividly remembers the day she arrived in the valley to start her new job. 'It was Alwinton Show Day, the second Saturday in October, and I came up the valley in my little blue van with two sheepdogs in the back, and the policemen at the entrance to the show waved me into the car park thinking I was going to the show and I was too shy to say I wasn't. So when he wasn't looking I just turned round and came out of the car park and went on up the valley, because I just wanted to get to Blindburn. As I was settling into my house I remember seeing Stewart coming back from the show and taking his dogs for a walk in the heather across the bridge and I found myself thinking: this is a nice place.'

It wasn't just the place that she developed a liking for. Gwen and Stewart already knew one another from the year Gwen spent at college. Hers had been a particularly sociable group and Stewart, tall, good-looking and amusing, had been made welcome in their midst. But working as shepherds on a remote hill farm threw them together even more and it wasn't long before they were spending their spare time, as well as work time, together. They became engaged and set a date for the wedding. Then six weeks before the appointed day, disaster struck. Fire swept through their cottage at Blindburn.

Stewart recalls it vividly. At the time he, Gwen and the other shepherd who worked with them were clipping sheep at Makendon, a hill farm – now part of Blindburn – which lies a couple of miles further up the Coquet valley: 'The shepherd's wife at Blindburn saw the fire. She couldn't drive, but she stopped somebody on the road and they came up and told us the house was ablaze. By the time we got back we couldn't do anything about it. Luckily we got into the kitchen and brought out the Calor gas bottles, because if they'd caught hold there would have been no house left. As it was, it was just a shell.'

Everything the couple possessed was lost or destroyed, including Gwen's engagement ring, all their engagement presents and gifts which had arrived well in advance of the wedding. Stewart was particularly sad to lose some beautiful carved crooks and albums containing photographs of all his previous sheepdogs. Worst of all,

Gwen's carefully-chosen wedding dress and the suit Stewart was planning to get married in were ruined. 'The only things we had to wear were the clothes we stood up in,' he remembers. 'And it brings it all home to you how much you've lost when you realise that the only things you've got are your clipping clothes!'

Stewart, all six foot three of him, managed to find a replacement suit in a gents' outfitters in nearby Jedburgh. But it was a traditional family bridal shop called Armstrongs in the market town of Haltwhistle in west Northumberland which came to Gwen's rescue. Despite having very little time, they made her a wedding dress which was every bit as beautiful as the one which went up in smoke. And on September 1st 1990 the couple were married at a church in the nearby village of Otterburn in a wedding service which included – naturally – the hymn 'The Lord's My Shepherd'.

A national newspaper had heard of their plight when the cottage caught fire. The day after the wedding it ran a story under the headline 'Flames Can't Defeat Shepherds In Love' and a picture of the couple in front of their gutted house. The article underneath read: 'Two ravaged cottages stand testament to the love of Stewart Wallace and Gwen Roberts. The sweetheart shepherds yesterday made it to the altar against all the odds. Fire destroyed all their possessions – including their wedding outfits – six weeks before the big day…'

Friends and family had rallied round to help Gwen and Stewart after the fire. The newspaper did its bit, too. It arranged for them to start their married life in comfort – by spending their honeymoon in a top hotel in Aberdeen.

It took a while for Gwen's cottage to be re-built and re-equipped and in the first 12 months of their marriage the newlyweds lived in five different places, including two caravans.

'It was a year I'd like to forget,' Stewart admits. But finally, their home was ready and they could feel settled. 'I wanted to marry a rich farmer', Gwen jokes, 'and I ended up with a poor shepherd. But that's love.'

The way the work is divided up on Blindburn's 5,500 acres has depended on how many shepherds there were. When Gwen arrived there were two – Stewart and another man – looking after the farm's seven 'hirsels' (hills), each with its own name. 'I was given the herding on Yearning Hall and The Rigg,' Gwen says. 'Stewart had Makendon and the West Side and the other shepherd had three hirsels, East Side, Eild Rigg and Fulhope Edge. Then he retired and we did it between us.'

On a farm carrying so many sheep it's just not possible to recognise every animal in the way shepherds did when they cared for smaller flocks a hundred years ago. But sometimes a sheep lodges itself in the affections of the shepherds. Edna the Blackface ewe was one, arriving in 1996. 'That was an awfully wet year at lambing time and we ended up with a lot of pet lambs,' remembers Gwen. 'One of them was Edna. She was a good lamb and we decided to keep her as a breeding sheep and she's turned out well, producing at least one lamb every year until now. She was always a determined character and she liked to stay at home, not go out onto the fell. One year she was away on summer grazing when she jumped a couple of fences, with her lamb right behind her, and ended up among some sheep belonging to our neighbour, who also had sheep on grass parks at the same place. Unbeknown to us, she must have come back in a wagon to our neighbour's place up in the hills because one day there she was, back at our door, with her lamb, both of them having jumped the cattle grid to get back home!'

In the summer months after lambing time, when the shepherds' job is to patrol their patch and check on their ewes and lambs, Gwen developed a routine which included calling in on a remote bothy on the top of Lamb Hill, 1,677 feet above sea level, where walkers can shelter if they're caught in a storm. Named the Yearning Saddle rescue hut, the wooden refuge is located at a key point on the 250-mile national trail, the Pennine Way. It has three benches just wide enough to sleep on and many hikers choose to stay the night there and break the challenging 25-mile stretch between Byrness and Kirk Yetholm. 'If anyone was spending the night it must have been a bit of a rude awakening to have a shepherdess and her dogs knocking on the door at seven o'clock in he morning,' Gwen laughs. In the hut there's a book signed by everyone who passes through and Gwen would add her name to the list, signing it 'Gwen Wallace, shepherdess' and putting 'resident' in the address column! 'Sometimes I might also meet the neighbouring shepherd from the Scottish side, Peter Tweedie, whose land joins Blindburn at the Border, and we'll have a chat and exchange snippets of news. When you're working in such an isolated place it's great to run into a friend in the middle of nowhere.'

Feminists might object to the use of the term 'shepherdess' but Gwen doesn't mind the description. 'To be honest,' she says, 'I prefer shepherdess to shepherd, because if someone says I'm a shepherd they might think I'm a lad.' She laughs, 'Being small, I'm sometimes mistaken for one, I have to admit. But anyway I like the word shepherdess. It's not a problem, because I work with Stewart my husband, and he's not going to be sexist to me, and of course I've got a woman boss.'

Gwen is grateful for the time she's spent in this majestic but often lonely corner of the country. 'It's been a great learning experience', she says. 'I've picked up a lot from Stewart about dogs and about sheep. The college gave me the basics, which is what you're hoping they'll do. But I think I've learned more from running my own dogs at Blindburn and working with my husband.'

In her 15 years in the Cheviot Hills, Gwen's modes of transport have changed. 'Initially I didn't have anything mechanical and I walked everywhere. Then we got an old horse, Mollie, who was really nice, a bit slow, but that was all right for me. I herded on her for quite a while. She was great for the dogs because they could go at her pace. But when she got old it was difficult to get a replacement, a horse you could really trust on the hill. I wouldn't pretend that I'm an experienced horse rider, and there's always the problem of them wandering off. Mollie was a little pest, you had to watch her like a hawk. And finding somewhere to tie her up with the reins wasn't always easy on the bare hill. There is one thing with a horse, though, it's quite nice in the snow. If your feet are cold you can get off and walk. You can't do that on a motorbike. I walk everywhere at lambing time and I love that. The rest of the time I use a quad bike.'

Stewart has six sheepdogs of varying ages and Gwen five. She reckons different jobs on the farm call for different dogs. 'At lambing time I use two dogs, one in the morning and another at night, because I think if you just stuck to the one dog they'd be knackered. And besides, you want to broaden their experience.'

Following her as she goes round the kennels at feeding time, you realise how utterly devoted Gwen is to her dogs – and what a handful a working pack can be. Each has its own distinct character, some shy, some extrovert, some noisy, some quiet. As Gwen spoons out food to each dog, eagerly waiting in its kennel, she lists each one in turn.

Brown-coated Kim is a five-year-old Australian kelpie, a daughter of Stewart's kelpie, Amy. 'She's the noisy one that barks. Kelpies do that. Bark and bark. She would make a lovely pet, as she's great when she's in the house. I couldn't do a lambing with her, but she's useful for some things. She's good in the pens, especially when we're putting sheep up into the wagon. She barks and gets the sheep to respond. She's really just a different breed of dog and I was intrigued to see how she would be.'

Jess is Gwen's oldest dog, a Border Collie like the rest. She's rising nine. She's treasured by Gwen because she's the mother of her three-year-old bitch, Jill. 'I really like Jill. She's really the first I've bred and trained and trialled, so I'm very fond of her. She's easily handled and she's getting better and better, except when she goes to the trials, when she gets excited. But hopefully she'll mature.'

Next in the pack comes Zak, aged two, who is also earmarked for sheepdog-trial work. And then there's Bob, with his bobtail, the short-tailed Collie. 'He's a year old, and he's just starting to work,' Gwen says. 'The tail's not a problem, it doesn't stop him working, he tucks it in so that you can't see it. I suppose if I took him to a dog trial there'd be some comments, because he's no show dog. But I'm confident he'll turn out well.'

Shepherds vary in their dog-training techniques and Gwen is no exception. 'Everyone has their own method,' she explains. 'You need to see what the character of the dog is first. I think you have to start at an early age, teach them to come back to you. That's the most important thing, because you want the dog to enjoy coming back to you; it wants to be a pleasurable experience for it to do that. The last thing you want is the dog out of control with you running after it. When they're pups, we have them in the house, and we keep calling them back. Or, when you go out, have one on a long lead and then keep calling it back, get them to sit and stay, and praise them when they do. Some dogs like to lie and others like to sit, and I wouldn't pressure them to lie if they don't want to. You can buy a book which tells you how to train a dog, but I've had quite a lot of pups and you learn most from that. Some dogs you can't start at six or seven months, you don't want to put too much pressure on them, so you have to wait a bit longer. It's difficult to explain, because every dog's different. Like human beings, they've got different characters. But they're all very rewarding.'

For Gwen and Stewart, shopping trips have to be carefully planned. From where they live it's ten miles to the nearest village and a further couple of miles to a post office. The nearest market town, with its supermarkets, clothes shops and hairdressers, is more than 20 miles away. The postmen used to bring newspapers with them when they delivered mail up the valley, but that service ended several years ago. And the days when butcher's and baker's vans called are long gone.

In terms of evening entertainment, though, the area has more to offer than you might have expected. Gwen and Stewart play carpet bowls at the village hall, and there's a dominoes school and a pool league at one of the pubs, where Stewart also chalks the scores for the ladies' darts team.

However, it's the dogs that dominate the majority of their lives. Every weekend from the end of May to the second week in October there are sheepdog trials in Northumberland. Gwen and Stewart try to compete in them all. 'We love it,' Gwen says. 'We've both got dogs we are training to run better and the only way to test them is to go to the trials. We see people we know every week, which is nice when you're working a long way away from anybody else.'

On the question of holidays, Gwen smiles. 'They tend to be a bit of a busman's holiday. We go to sheepdog trials.' However, this devotion to a common theme does not always result in marital bliss. 'A couple of years ago we went to Northern Ireland for the international sheepdog trials,' laughs Gwen. 'There was nearly a divorce! The trials only last for three days but we had rented a cottage for a week. We were totally bored the rest of the time. There wasn't much to do and we didn't have the dogs with us. We missed taking them for walks…'

5 Stewart Wallace

*B*oys grow up fast when they're faced with an emergency. Stewart Wallace was just 14 when his father and older brother, both shepherds on the farm where they lived, were struck low by a severe bout of flu at lambing time. With no one else to call on, the farmer who employed them turned to Stewart, recognising that he had the ability to take over. 'Up to that time, I loved woodwork,' he says. 'My dream was to become a joiner. But that lambing time changed all that. Morning, noon and night I worked with the sheep and I just got bitten by the bug. From then on, that was going to be the life for me.'

Few birthdays stand out more in Stewart's memory than his 16th. It was the day when he left the classroom and the exercise book behind and entered the adult world of work. 'Can I recall going into school for the last time?' he says. 'Yes, I remember it well. It was a Tuesday morning, 23 February. I had to go round all my class teachers to get them to sign a form, and then I went to see the headmaster. It all took less than half an hour. I suppose I could have stopped there all day if I'd wanted to, but I just wanted to put school behind me.

'I got home at about 11 o'clock. I knew they'd be busy in the sheep folds. Without a thought I jumped straight in, still wearing my school trousers, and started to help. I can remember coming in for my dinner and my mother standing there, looking at me.

'She said: "I see you've been working with the sheep again."

'I said, "Aye".

'"But you've got your school trousers on!"

'"It doesn't matter. I'm not going back to school. I'll not be needing them again."

'And that was it. I started work that afternoon as an assistant shepherd.

'My first week's wage was £28 a week, of which my mother got £10 for board and lodging and my father got £2 for the keep of my dogs. It's always been a set thing on the farms: board and lodgings, and dog-food allowance, and I was left with £14 a week. But you know something? In many ways I was better off then than I am today. When you got paid £14 a week it went a long, long way in those days.'

The responsibility thrust onto him at an early age may have made Stewart mature more quickly than some. There is a kindness and composure about the tall shepherd that makes people warm to him straight away. After I'd first contacted his employer, Judith, to ask if we could film her shepherds at work, Stewart was only too happy to show me the full extent of the land he patrolled. As we stood at a point high on the border between Scotland and England the setting sun bathed the Cheviot Hills in a yellow light. It was a peaceful scene, but Stewart gently reminded me that it wasn't always so serene. I would feel very different at this altitude in a white-out.

Stewart was born on 23 February, 1961, in Simpson's Memorial Hospital in Edinburgh. At the time his father and mother lived at a farm called New Heighton, which is three or four miles outside Coldstream in Berwickshire. Theirs was a familiar picture of employment in the Scottish Borders: Stewart's father was a shepherd on the farm and his mother worked in the big house as a cleaner.

'When we left New Heighton in 1966 my father moved to a job at Corsbie near Earlston in Berwickshire but we were only there about a year. My father didn't see eye to eye with the boss at the time and so he left and got a job at Hoselaw, which is half-way between Yetholm and Kelso. From there I went to Yetholm Primary School and Kelso High School until I left school in 1977.

'I'm the ninth of ten, with five brothers and four sisters. I've got two brothers who farm for themselves, one's a shepherd like me, one drives a tractor for a chemical spray company and one trains people to drive buses in Manchester.

'My father was still working at Hoselaw when I started, but he was 65 and due to retire. He said he would stay on an extra year to help me get established, which he did. To my father, there were two ways to do a job: you could do it his way, or you could do it the wrong way. Ninety-five per cent of the time his way was the right way. But some of the time he was wrong, yet he would never, ever admit it.

'We didn't fall out. But at times we had what you might call heated discussions when we were working together in the sheep pens. Not that it made much difference, arguing with him. I don't recall him ever losing an argument.'

When his father finally hung up his crook after 50 years as a shepherd, Stewart, then 17, was, as he puts it, thrown in at the deep end. He did the shepherding job at Hoselaw for three years on his own. He was still living at home, looked after by his mother and he was conscious that his father would be watching him at work, even though he'd retired. But it was an enjoyable time.

'At Hoselaw you got up, had a cup of tea, fed the dogs and set off at seven o'clock. You could look across to the top of Cheviot, so Hoselaw seemed to be high up. But it was all in-bye – not hill – land. The farm carried 750 greyfaced ewes. With a thousand acres of in-bye ground it was a big area to look after sheep in and it would be ten o'clock before I landed back in.'

Keen though he'd been to end his general education at school, Stewart recognised there might be value in getting some specialised training in agriculture. 'I went to college on day release when I was at Hoselaw, a three-year course which amounted to 25 days in the year. The first year we did grass management, the second year we did cattle and the third year sheep. But by the time I got to the third year I'd been working on a farm for three years and I knew almost everything that was being taught. That's not to say I didn't benefit from the course. It was useful in many ways – and it gave me a qualification.'

Stewart passed the exams and was chosen as the top practical student in his year. Meanwhile, however, a cloud fell over his job; he was made redundant from Hoselaw and had to cast around for work. Through a friend of his father's, a contact from the sheep-dog world, he found employment on a farm at Denholm near Hawick where a shepherd was needed to do the in-bye (lowland) lambing from mid-March to mid-April. And, in the custom of contract shepherding, he followed that up from mid-April to mid-May with a hill lambing at Featherwood Farm, on the Ministry of Defence ranges near Otterburn in Northumberland. The family asked him if he would like to work there full-time and he stayed for three years. 'I'd never worked with Blackface sheep until I went to Featherwood. They had what we call the Northumberland type of Blackface, the Hexham type, big, long sheep that need a good bit of looking after in the winter. It was a new experience for me, being on a real hill farm.'

In 1984 Stewart moved again and started work for Judith Ridley, tenant of Blindburn at the head of the valley of the River Coquet, the biggest unit on the ranges. It's really two farms run together, Blindburn and Makendon, comprising 5,500 acres and carrying nearly 2,000 ewes, mainly Blackfaces. 'The farm has a good reputation,' he says. 'It's well-known for its stock. I heard on the grapevine there was a vacancy, so I rang up, had an interview and got the job. I've been here ever since. Twenty years, give or take a couple of months.'

Like many flocks on high ground in Britain, Blindburn's is made up of 'hefted' or 'heafed' sheep, a special term which is thought to be derived from the old Nordic word 'hefta' meaning 'to bind'. Over centuries hefted sheep have acquired the extraordinary ability to remain on specific areas of the hills without straying. It's an instinct lambs learn from their mothers. From time to time hefted sheep are gathered off their own piece of ground and driven down from the hills to be given some attention in the handling pens at the farm. But as soon as they're released their natural homing impulse guides them back to their own hefts.

'The sheep on the farm are all born and bred on the hill,' says Stewart. 'Their mothers and their grandmothers have been there for generations before them, and they're hefted to their own bit of ground. They remain there for the rest of their breeding lives.' Some say that over the years hefted sheep build up a greater resistance to the diseases, especially those transmitted by ticks, which might be present on that particular piece of land. But the main purpose of hefting is to spread the grazing over the whole area covered by the farm. If they weren't programmed to stay on their own hefts the sheep would constantly be drawn to the best parts of the hill which would become overgrazed to the detriment of the rest of the farm.

When foot and mouth disease cast a huge shadow over British farming in 2001 large numbers of hefted sheep were slaughtered on the orders of Defra, to the dismay of flockmasters. However, Defra eventually agreed to give hefted sheep exemption from the culls, accepting that they represented a valuable gene pool which should be preserved at all costs. Three years on from the agony of FMD, schemes are in place to 're-heft' some areas where hefted sheep were removed and culled, but it remains to be seen how successful they will be.

Stewart is just relieved that his part of Northumberland escaped. 'I would hate to think what would have happened if we had got foot and mouth here because hefting takes a lot of time and effort,' he says. 'Unless you've got the whole hill fenced in it's all open ground and it can take months and months. You've got to be with the sheep most of the time, keeping them on that bit of ground, making sure they don't wander.'

One agricultural commentator, writing in 1906, wryly remarked: 'Let anyone start a flock where the old hefted flock has been sold off and if he did not know before what the hardships of penal servitude were he will soon learn. To heaf sheep above two years old is as near an impossibility as I have known. Even when fences are good, sheep fail to settle. They pine and fret and do not thrive as native sheep do.'

The story goes that when sheep were originally being hefted (or 'bound on', as some call it) the shepherds slept on the fells with them for months. In between keeping them on their allotted ground, they built the 'stells' (sheepfolds) that are scattered over the hills. These are small stonewall enclosures with an opening at one side where sheep may find shelter in a storm. It's said that, over the centuries, a circular design proved to be better than a square because in a blizzard the snow swirled into the round stell and out again, whereas the square quickly filled up. Many stells have collapsed over the years and are now just heaps of stones, but in some places they have been carefully preserved. A few are located close to a farm steading where, in the old days, they were put to a different use during the summer. The floors of the stell were so deep in sheep dung that shepherds used to grow their potato crops in them!

Different stonewall shelters, H-shaped or S-shaped, can still be seen in remote glens in Scotland. Careful thought was given to where these should be positioned so as to give sheep the best possible chance when the weather deteriorated. Their design meant that sheep could huddle together on either side of the wall depending on which way the wind was blowing.

The language of the countryside can be confusing. Stewart's noticed it, too. He's intrigued as to why sheep-handling complexes have such a range of different names. In England they're known as pens, folds or sheepcotes. In his native Berwickshire they're called 'faulds'. And throughout the rest of Scotland they're referred to as 'fanks'. Another term used by shepherds in the North of England and Scotland is 'hirsel'. It means an area of land on a hill farm on which sheep are hefted, and which has its own name. On each hirsel, depending on the size, there are a number of 'cuts', or groups, of sheep numbering 100 or thereabouts. They are also identified by name.

Blindburn there are seven different hirsels. Two carry just a single cut of sheep. Three hirsels have two cuts of sheep on them. And two have three cuts of sheep on them. It sounds complicated, I know. But it means that when the shepherds wants to mark the new lambs, for instance, they gather a cut of sheep at a time instead of gathering the whole hill in one go. When they've finished, the sheep go back to the area where they were born and bred.

Hill farms retain a quarter of their ewe lambs each year to come into the flock as replacements for the 'draft' (aged) ewes. Selecting these lambs at weaning (in Scotland, 'speaning' or 'spaining') time is a real skill. Only the very best must be selected to maintain the quality of the stock.

As for the sheep, how do the shepherds know which old ewes are due to go? Well, on most hill farms the last number of the year they were born is branded on the base of the horn. If they're born in 2003 that means it's the figure 3, so it's simple to work out the age of an individual animal.

The ewes are normally 'drafted' at six-years-old, so when the sheep are being sorted the shepherds check the number on the horns. As well as that, they examine the ewes' mouths. If they still have their eight teeth they go as top draft ewes and will almost certainly command a better price from lowland farmers hoping to get at least one more lamb crop out of them. But if they've lost some teeth they're sold as 'warranted in udder only', which means their ability to feed themselves is impaired – but they can still produce milk and raise lambs.

The length of a ewe's life depends to a large extent on whether she has teeth to feed herself with. In the 1970s a dentist who had connections with the farming industry experimented with fitting a kind of brace to sheep's teeth to enable them to keep munching and therefore increase their longevity. But because of the cost of the treatment in relation to the value of the ewe, it didn't catch on. The same problem surrounds the use of vets in sheep flocks. At one time, farmers would summon a vet to help with a difficult birth, but today that only happens when the sheep are pedigree animals and therefore particularly valuable. In most cases the vet's call-out fee is greater than the sheep's value.

On a small number of hill farms the ewe lambs retained for breeding ('ewe hoggs') remain on the farm over their first winter. But their owners don't want them to be mated by rams running with the ewes in the rest of the flock because it's considered that the hoggs are not mature enough to withstand the trauma of pregnancy and birth. Besides, there's a risk of them being tupped by their own father. So in the past shepherds would attempt to take preventative measures. The animals were 'breeked' by sewing a piece of cloth or sacking over the hogg's tail-head to block an amorous ram's advances. The usual choice of material for this birth control measure was unbleached calico, and staff at haber-dasher shops in country towns knew exactly what was meant when shepherds' wives called in to order some in the autumn of the year.

Historians Clive Dalton and Donald Clegg recall one farm in the 1940s where the 'breeks' were pieces of tweed made from the farm's own wool. And those being hard times, there was no wastage, either. At the end of the 'tupping' (mating) season the breeking was removed, washed and stored for use the following year! As to the effectiveness of such a contraceptive device, Donald Clegg doubts whether it was always 100 per cent successful. 'Nature being what it is,' he reports, 'some tups always found a way.'

The practice has almost died out now, but Stewart remembers

it being used at Featherwood Farm when he worked there in the early 1980s. 'I breeked many a hogg at that place,' he says. 'I used to enjoy it. It was freezing cold in November but we were keeping warm in the shed. It was an old-fashioned way of doing things, but I didn't mind it at all.'

As on many hill and upland farms, the Blindburn hoggs spend their first winter in the comparative comfort of an 'in-bye' farm. 'Our boss has rented land in-bye for many years and we winter our hoggs on that ground. They come back a lot fitter and stronger,' Stewart explains.

People argue about the shepherd's year and when it begins. Is it when lambs arrive in the spring? Is it when they go to the lamb sales in the autumn? Many contend it starts when the rams are introduced to the ewes. But before that happens, Stewart's employer Judith and her son Matthew, who have purchased new Blackface and Swaledale rams to run with the flock, have to decide which rams will go where. To avoid in-breeding, rams spend no more that two consecutive years with one group of ewes before being put in with another group, and with seven hirsels (hills) on the farm, by moving the rams around, there's scope to use them throughout their lives, so long as they stay healthy.

For each hirsel the rams are given a colour mark on a different place on their fleece, signifying that's where they belong this year. The positions on the ram's body where the marks are made have names handed down over generations; for example, black pop on the near rib, red pop on the far rib, red pop on the far hook. It's a complicated series of marks for shepherd and farmer to remember, but fortunately everything is written down, including rams' ear tag numbers, in a log book.

Rams are put out with the ewes on the 20th November, which means the flock will start lambing on around the 15th of April. Rams at tupping time can stray and get into fights, sometimes with fatal consequences, so ensuring they remain with their allotted ewes is part of the shepherd's job. 'They may be tempted to stray,' Stewart says, 'but on three hirsels they're in enclosures so they can't, and the other hirsel's right in front of the house and if a tup's strayed onto it I just fetch him back to the place where he belongs'.

When lambing starts Matthew looks after the ewes on Makendon and the West Side, and the shepherds take care of the remainder.

In the autumn decisions have to be made about which lambs are to be sold, and where. Sometimes one of the best Blackface wethers (male lambs) is retained to use as a ram in the flock, but the remaining Blackface wether lambs are sent to the mart, along with ewe lambs not needed as replacements. Meanwhile, elderly ewes are sent to the draft ewe sales. Cheviot rams are used on the Blackface ewes to mop up those missed by the Blackface rams during the first few weeks of tupping time, and their cross-bred lambs are fattened and sold in prime stock sales.

Shepherds always seem to have a large number of dogs barking furiously in the kennels at the approach of strangers. Stewart is no exception, but, as with all aspects of hill shepherding, there is a reason. Some are just young and are still being trained, and some are over the hill. 'I have six dogs, of which two are retired now that they're 12-years-old. One of them's a kelpie called Amy. I bought her for £150. She wasn't a great gathering dog, but once she had sheep in a heap she was back and forward the whole time; a great worker. My other old one is Meg. She's been my trial dog for the last ten years. She's a super trial bitch. I've run her every year and I've always won a prize with her. It's just a pity old age has caught up with her. Both Amy and Meg can still do a wee bit with the sheep, but I rely on the younger ones for that.

'Next is a dog I bought in 2001, Joey. She's a white-headed little bitch who doesn't like strangers and I have to admit I wouldn't always trust her. I think she would bite, given the chance. She's a good little work bitch, if you want anything caught in a field, she's the one to ask. Then there's Marie, a bitch I bought last year to replace my trial bitch. She's getting better as the months go on and she's going like a train at the minute. She's four.

'Then there's Ben, who we bred ourselves out of Gwen's bitch. I sent him as a pup to a friend and bought him back at six months old. He must be one of the horniest dogs I've ever had. If any of the bitches are in season, he's hard to control. But he's a super hill dog. I can put him out any distance so long as he can hear me, and if he's cutting in at the sheep I can stop him there and tell him to look and he'll stop and look. He's not keen at driving sheep away from you at the minute but I've never forced him. I'm sure he's got it in him.

'The last one is little Jed. She's a sister to Ben and just a year old. Unlike him, she's timid but she's going to be a good work dog. I've never pushed her. But she's getting better all the time.

'I like to have a pup most years and if I don't need it myself I'll sell it on. I like breeding a litter of pups. I get great enjoyment out of bringing them on. In the time we've been here I've bred a lot of pups that have gone away to be trial dogs. The most successful was Spot, who was bought by one of our leading local handlers, Paul Turnbull, and who twice got into the English team at the national sheepdog trials.

'The only reason I take a litter of pups is for myself. It's not done commercially. Besides, there's not a lot of money in it. Last year we had a litter of six. If we had sold all six for £100 each that would have been £600. But I kept a pup and Gwen kept a pup so that's your return cut to £400. Powdered milk and puppy food cost about £100, the stud fee was £100 and the registration fee was £74, so you're down to £126 profit. It's a lot of work for not much money.'

Soon after he arrived at Blindburn Stewart moved into one of the two south-facing farm cottages which stand next to the big farm-house, overlooking the Coquet. What with breeding sheepdogs and his interest in sheepdog trials, his was very much a bachelor life – until Gwen came along. 'Gwen was a student at the local agricultural college, Kirkley Hall. They have the farm next to us, Carlcroft, and I'd seen her there. A lass on the same course as Gwen came and did a lambing here. She was very friendly with Gwen and I got invitations to various discos at Kirkley Hall. I got to know all the students that year. There were about 15 of them. But for me, Gwen stood out.

'When a job became vacant here at lambing time, Judith, my boss, put an advert up at Kirkley Hall. Gwen finished at the college in the July and went back home to Anglesey, but there was no chance of a job down there. Then she remembered seeing the advert for job up at Blindburn. It was still vacant. So she applied for it and moved here in the October – Alwinton Show day, 1988. The rest is history. We lived in the two farm cottages, side by side, for about 18 months. We just got to know each other through work and liked each other. So we decided to get married.'

Stewart adds, 'Mind you, it was handy she lived next door. I don't believe in spending a lot of money travelling great distances when I'm courting!' But there's a twinkle in his eyes when he says it – and you know that if he'd had to pursue Gwen much further afield, distance would have been no object!

6 Spring

∽

Shepherd's Harvest

Lambing time conjures up an image of happy lambs gambolling in the spring sunshine. While that's often the picture in May, when the countryside is throwing off its winter clothes and the grass is growing again, the previous two months can be a time of toil and trouble for shepherds. Whether lambing takes place in parks, pens, or on open grazing they need to be at hand to keep an eye on the proceedings and carry out their roles as midwives – or even vets.

Dave's off to check the sheep long before breakfast and as soon as he goes through the gate into a lambing field he spots the day's first patient, a Blackface ewe. Only one of her teats is giving milk and she's in some discomfort with a swollen udder. With softly-spoken commands to his dogs Nap and Scott, the shepherd carefully corners the ewe and grabs her round the neck with his crook. Her lamb hovers close by as she's turned onto her backside. Soon milk is being stripped from the bulging bag in deft squeezes, much to the relief of the sheep. 'She should have had two lambs, given the quantity of milk she's got,' says Dave, 'but as it is, she's just got a single and she's only suckling it on one side. The lamb can't cope with the amount of milk, so I'll just have to drain her off for a day or two. It would end up with trouble if I didn't doctor her.'

The ewe is five-years-old and this is her last lambing on the hill. Come October she'll be sold as a 'draft' ewe in the autumn sheep sales and will spend the rest of her breeding life on a lowland farm. Dave doesn't know all the sheep individually; that would be impossible with some 800 ewes, not to mention the 200 ewe hoggs retained as replacements. But in this instance he does recognise the sheep. 'I had the same trouble with her last year,' says Dave. 'Having a large udder's a fault with some of these ewes. Sometimes you'll get a lamb that only wants to suck one side, and that can be the cause of the problem.' As the milk jets onto the grass from the teat Dave's draining, he smiles. 'Takes us back to the days when I used to milk the cows by hand.'

A new-born lamb lies in the grass, the afterbirth (placenta) a couple of feet away. A ewe is walking away from the scene, followed by two other tiny lambs. A few paces further down the field stand half a dozen ewes, some with lambs and some without. It's a classic test of the shepherd's powers of observation – and of his experience. Which sheep is the mother of the new-born lamb? And are those two lambs staggering after the other ewe her twins, or two singles from other mothers? Dave leans on his stick, watching patiently; the dogs wait at a distance; the minutes pass. The lamb tries to suckle one of the ewes and is butted away. 'That's not her lamb, then,' he murmurs to himself. 'But which one is?' Eventually, with a great deal of baaing and bleating, the right lambs find their mothers.

Dave moves through the flock, controlling the dogs in a low

voice. For a while now he's been carrying a lamb. He doesn't want to get his scent onto it, so he's holding it by its legs. It's a twin, but the mother has shown little interest in it. If it doesn't find a source of milk, it will die. The only answer is to try to get another ewe to foster it. Dave spots a sad, but not uncommon, sight in the lee of a wall at the end of the field: a ewe standing over her still-born lamb. She'll have plenty of milk, but no lamb to drink it. It presents the shepherd with an opportunity to save one small life.

Not far away is a triangular pen made of three metal hurdles. It was put there in the sure knowledge that problems would occur in lambing time and a temporary 'isolation ward' would come in useful. As his dogs direct the bereft ewe into the pen, Dave collects the dead lamb and, using his pen-knife, begins to strip the skin off it. Swiftly the coat is removed from the forlorn carcass and slipped over the body of the rejected twin, and blood from the dead animal wiped on the live lamb's head. That, and the woolly jacket, will fool the ewe into thinking the lamb is hers. The lamb is placed in the pen beside its 'mother'. Leaving it with her in the confines of the small enclosure for the next few hours will – it's hoped – make her accept it. It's called 'setting on' a lamb in these parts. 'There are other ways to set a lamb on but I think the skin is the best with these hill ewes,' Dave says, watching to see how the ewe is taking to the lamb. 'Really, the best place to do it is where she's dropped her dead lamb because she knows from the smell that's where her lamb is. Shifting her from where she gave birth and putting her in a pen, as I did, might have upset her. We'll have to wait and see. You do your best. She seems to be quite settled with it. Hopefully by nightfall she'll be out of the pen and away with the lamb.'

On his way home for breakfast, Dave makes a short detour along a track overlooking a shallow valley. He's hoping it's still early enough in the day to witness a very special moorland sight. The heather grows thickly over most of the area, but between some rocks and a small conifer plantation there's a bare patch. Dave's lucky. A dozen beautiful birds are deeply preoccupied in showing off their plumage to one another and uttering strange hissing sounds. This is a 'lek' and the birds engaged in their traditional springtime display are male black grouse. From where Dave's standing, they do look all black, as their name suggests. But through his binoculars he's able to appreciate the red wattle above the birds' eyes and their remarkable white-centred, lyre-shaped tails.

Buzzing to and fro with their feathers raised, the blackcocks are hoping to see off their rivals while at the same time attracting the attention of the female birds, known as 'grey hens' because of their rather nondescript grey-brown plumage. Nationally, black grouse are declining in numbers, but in this part of Northumberland populations seem to be healthy. 'I like to see them,' Dave says. 'It's one of the signs of spring. They come back to the same lek year after year and I think it's fascinating the way they display. Each one's just trying to reign supreme!'

After breakfast – always a moveable feast in the uncertain weeks of lambing time – Dave and his sheepdogs are off to another part of the farm to check on some more Blackface ewes that are due to lamb. This time the maternity ward is a big field next to the River Coquet. The sounds of birds returning after the winter complement the noise of the sheep. Oyster-catchers are among the first visitors, their unmistakable cleep-cleep-cleep calls ringing out as they wheel over the valley. And groups of common sandpipers are back again, busily flying to and fro along the river-side gravel beds.

Some of the ewes have given birth to twins and Dave wants to move them and their tiny lambs to a field nearby where the grass is slightly better. It also makes it easier to keep an eye on the remainder. Nick and Scott are at their best, carefully splitting the in-lamb ewes from those that have lambed and guiding the latter through a gate into the vacant field. 'A good dog on a sheep farm is like a joiner with a hammer,' Dave says. 'It's a necessity. If you haven't got a good dog you may as well give up.' But he would be the first to agree that some sheepdogs are less suitable than others for this particular job. 'You have to be gentle with the sheep at lambing time,' Dave says. 'You don't want to be working with a robust kind of dog. You want one that's sensible.'

The weather is a major factor in limiting the number of lambs that survive. 'It's everything, isn't it?' Dave says. 'If the weather's good the lambs will get to their feet and are able to look after themselves. If it's bad you have a hard time. Lambs seem to be able to cope with dry, frosty days, but sleet is real killing weather. They're only little when they're born. They can take a lot, but they can't stand being wet and cold.' The local expression for lambs suffering from hypothermia is 'starving', and 'starvation' is the term used to describe raw, icy conditions. Understandably, the words are a regular part of shepherds' vocabulary in lambing time.

In the warmth of his house Dave watches the weather forecasts on television. But he takes the view that as far as lambing's concerned there's not much you can do to change things. 'Whether it's wet, dry, rain or snow, it comes, anyway.' He may be fatalistic about the weather, but some hill shepherds pray for a spell of bad weather at the beginning of March, bearing in mind the saying that if March 'comes in like a lion, it will go out like a lamb', and hoping they will be blessed by fine days during lambing. The gestation period of ewes is five months. In the hills, rams aren't put out with the ewes until mid-November, so that it will be April before the peak of lambing time is reached. It's hoped that, by then, the worst of the winter will be over.

On some 'in-bye' farms ewes spend lambing time in sheds or in temporary accommodation such as polytunnels or marquees. In warm pens deep in straw, such flocks avoid the vagaries of the weather. Round-the-clock monitoring of the sheep is done by members of the farmer's family or by their staff and lambing percentages (the number of live lambs per a hundred ewes) are much higher.

Of course, many lowland farms lamb their sheep in fields, a less expensive option and one which, some claim, is better for the sheep's health because infections don't spread so easily. For shepherds watching outdoor lowland flocks, caravans are still used in some places, although naturally they're more comfortable than they were a hundred years ago. At that time a shepherd's 'mobile home' was often a corrugated iron hut mounted on wheels which was drawn by horse to the field just before lambing began. Furnished in very basic fashion with a bunk, a wooden table and a bench, the hut usually had a cast-iron stove for heating and cooking. Some sheep farming areas like Romney Marsh in Kent, where the shepherds were known as 'lookers', had purpose-built brick huts where shepherds lived. Only a few of these structures have survived, prompting calls to have them listed as historic buildings.

A more basic version of a shepherd's refuge was in the lee of a thorn thicket. These bushes were clipped and lined with straw to make a hideaway for shepherds and it's said that Shepherds Bush in London was the site of one such shelter in times gone past.

Late afternoon sees Dave out on another area of the farm called the North Side. 'Aye,' Dave says, 'it's well named the North Side. Sometimes the winds seem to come straight from Siberia.' As he strides towards the top of the hill Dave talks about the vegetation on this particular hill. It consists mainly of common bent, a prolific member of the agrostis genus of moorland grasses which grow in tufts and provide good grazing for sheep. Up to 50 years ago shepherds used to cut the bent and make it into hay. It dried quickly and was gathered into small stacks which, thatched with rushes, were placed at strategic points around the fell to provide emergency feed in storms. Hills are described as 'white' (mainly bent) or 'black' (mainly heather). 'This is the only white ground on the farm,' Dave explains. 'The rest is all black.'

As is the case on many other hill farms, including those listed elsewhere in this book, the Blackface sheep on the North Side are 'hefted' or 'bound on' to this particular part of the farm. They belong to it, it's their home and if moved away they would find their way back. 'They were born and bred on this piece of land, and their foremothers before them were born here too,' Dave says. In line with hill shepherding traditions going back at least 200 years, these sheep are 'raked' twice a day. In the morning they are brought down the hill by the shepherd and his dogs, and at night they are shifted back up, so that they lie out on the tops when it gets dark. The purpose of raking the flock is to prevent grazing being concentrated on one part of the fell. But at lambing time it offers an opportunity to review the sheep at close quarters. 'In the morning you push them to the bottom and you get your troubles at the top,' Dave says, 'and at night you drive them to the top and you've got your troubles at the bottom.' By troubles, he means a difficult lambing, a mis-mothering or a casualty.

Accompanying Dave is Natalie, his granddaughter, and a friend of hers, Jennifer. As they climb the hill they spot a lamb by itself, bleating plaintively. The other sheep are steadily making their way uphill but the lamb gets it into its head that its mother is down the hill and sets off in that direction. Dave has no other choice but to send Nap after it. The lamb, though only a few days old, is nimble but as the dog closes in it submits and Jennifer is able to run and pick it up.

'It had been lying sleeping and it woke up after its mother had gone with the rest of the sheep. Usually in that situation the mother comes back and collects the lamb. But I wasn't sure she was going to. The other ewes aren't interested in it. They know their own lambs and that's it. They just bump another lamb off. So I sent the dog to catch it.

'If you don't have a dog that can catch a lamb you can be in trouble. I have a dog, an old one, he won't catch a lamb. He won't even look at one. But both the dogs I've got today will. I had a bitch called Betty, she used to stop a lamb and gently put her foot on it. The lamb was just held there until you got hold of it. She was clever, Betty. If you need to 'set on' a lamb it's handy if you've got a dog that can catch one for you. Particularly when you're out on the fells.'

Jennifer places the lamb close to the sheep gathered on the crest of the hill and within a couple of minutes its mother emerges from the flock, calling for her youngster. They depart, reunited.

Some hill farms have no enclosed land and the ewes have to give birth to their lambs out on the hill. If they produce twins, the shepherd is faced with the bother of bringing them down to lower ground where there's better grazing, and where they can also be given more attention. There are some advantages of lambing on the hill, however. In many places there may be more protection from the elements among the rushes and rocks than there is in a fenced enclosure nearer to the farm steading. 'When I first started it was all lambing on the hill,' Dave says. 'It had its good points. When they were born on the hill they were used to obstacles like drains and they learned from their mothers where to cross them. But if they're born in enclosures they're more inclined to drop in the drains and drown.'

At the end of lambing, Dave sums it up like this: 'You're weary. But you feel as if you've achieved something. It's been worthwhile. It's your harvest.' He ponders the expression. 'Aye,' he says. 'That's the right way to put it. The lambs are your crop, and lambing time is your harvest.'

After 15 lambings at Blindburn, Gwen is comfortable with her routine. It's one that shepherds traditionally follow at lambing time. 'I go off to "look" the sheep first thing in the morning, before six o'clock, and see what problems there are, and then I come back in for breakfast. Then I might have a lamb to set on to a foster mother. In the afternoon we often have some sheep to move to different ground. Then I'll go back to the lambing ewes at about four o'clock and hopefully be back by seven. It all depends. Some evenings you can have a lot of problems and then you're in later.'

Walking purposefully through a group of sheep, she spots a ewe lying down. As she approaches it, with her dog Jill in close attendance, the sheep drags itself to its feet, but almost immediately keels over. It's got 'staggers', or hypomagnesaemia, a condition which can quickly become fatal. It's caused by a rapid fall in the level of magnesium in the ewe. Gwen takes a syringe from her rucksack and gives it an injection of a combined calcium and magnesium solution. 'It usually works,' she says, 'provided that you've caught it in time.'

Being there at the critical moment is so important at lambing time, but there never seems to be enough time. Often something goes wrong between the shepherd's early-morning round and the return visit in late afternoon. Gwen is ready for most eventualities, though. 'I carry a lambing survival kit. There's lubricant in case I have to help a ewe with a difficult birth. There's calcium. There's a colour spray aerosol to put numbers on the twins. Colostrum paste. String, that's an essential thing, to tie to a dead lamb and pull it along the ground, you give a little 'maaah' sound and the ewe follows you to a lambing paddock where you may be able to set her on with another lamb.'

Simple arithmetic can give a clue to something wrong. A group of ewes that have given birth to twins should obviously have an even number of lambs with them. If it's an odd number, a lamb has wandered off and needs to be found and returned to its mother – assuming she'll have it.

Then there's 'lamb-napping', sheep's own version of kidnapping. This is when a ewe pinches another one's lamb, usually before they've had their own. When theirs arrive, they may be twins which the thief either rejects, or is simply unable to rear. The solution is often to leave the ewe with the lamb she's stolen and one of her own, and 'set on' the third lamb to another mother. Then again, the ewe may refuse to keep the lamb she's pinched, once hers have arrived, in which case the shepherd has to find a mother for the stolen lamb. It can get very complicated and swift decisions have to be made. Even when they're heavily in lamb, ewes can move quickly and wrong-foot a pursuer. If a shepherd wants to catch them with a crook, it's important to make the first lunge pay or a chase ensues which can exhaust both the human and the animal.

Gwen notices a ewe struggling to give birth in a far-off corner of the field. It's hampered by a relatively common problem. The lamb's head and two front legs should be the first to show, but in this case, as happens all too often, one leg is tucked back. Gwen has to gently press the head back down the uterus, lock a finger behind the knee of the backward-lying leg and carefully pull the limb forward to the position for correct presentation. The lamb and its twin are born without any further complications. Malpresentations come in many different forms and the shepherds' skills are tested to the utmost. But there are feelings of relief and pleasure when they see the lambs shake their heads with their first few spluttering breaths and the mother licking and cleaning them.

'Every lambing time is different, with fresh challenges,' Gwen says. 'You're always drawing on your experience. But you're often learning something new too.'

But even when shepherds have done their best and succeeded in ushering tiny lambs into the world, outside forces can take a hand. Predators such as foxes, for instance, are a concern at lambing time. Weak lambs can be vulnerable, especially when a vixen is looking for food for her cubs. But one of the worst threats comes from the air in the shape of the 'corbie' (carrion crow). Usually alone, these all-black opportunists lurk close to pregnant ewes in the hope that a lamb may get stuck as it's emerging and they can peck out its eyes. The same gruesome treatment is meted out to a ewe if she turns over onto her back and is unable to right herself, as often happens when the animal is heavily pregnant. Within a short while, a corbie crow will target her eyes too. The 'hoodie' (hooded crow), which is found mainly in the North of Scotland, is an equally brutal and indiscriminate scavenger.

As Tennyson observed: Nature is red in tooth and claw.

✧

Healthy Sheep

Members of the pastoral community are wont to trot out the old saying: A sheep's worst enemy is another sheep. The inference is that over-stocking can build up health problems in flocks, and there may well be an element of truth in it. Certainly, Britain is keeping a lot more sheep than it used to, and old shepherds say many of them are 'too soft'.

The size of the national flock doubled from 20 million to 40 million in the 50 years between 1950 and 2000. And although the outbreak of foot and mouth disease in 2001 led to a dramatic decrease through the slaughter of 4.5 million sheep, a subsequent rise in prices tempted many farmers hit by the epidemic to re-stock, rather than give up sheep production altogether.

Of course, in the half century that has elapsed since 1950 the range of drugs available to flockmasters has increased dramatically. Nonetheless, there's some truth in another piece of farming lore: that a sheep's main aim in life is to die before you want it to. A glance at the number of ailments that can lay sheep low makes you wonder why any rational person would wish to keep them. Shepherds, of course, need to keep a constant watch on their animals to spot something going amiss before it's too late. Diseases of the blood, the breathing organs, the digestive system, the urinary organs, the nervous system, the eyes, the skin and the

Right: Stewart and Gwen on their wedding day. The marriage service hymns included 'The Lord Is My Shepherd'.

Below: After shepherding together for 15 years, Stewart and Gwen have a well-developed working relationship. 'We seem to know what needs to be done,' says Gwen. 'It's almost intuitive.'

Above: Top dogs: Gwen and Stewart with their leading Border Collies, Jill (with Gwen) and Ben. Most weekends from May to October the pair set off with their dogs to compete in sheepdog trials in the local area.

Left: Gwen says she's proud of her job title. 'Some people don't like the word, but I'm happy to be known as a shepherdess.'

Right: Bad weather at lambing time can bring problems. A lamb abandoned by its mother in an April storm has to be bottle fed by Gwen. For all its cuteness, a pet lamb is more a nuisance than a blessing. Wherever possible, the shepherd will try and get a ewe to adopt it, so it can be reared naturally.

Left: Starting young. Dave Baxter, aged nine, with his first sheepdog, Glen. 'I thought he was the best dog there'd ever been.'

Below: In complete control. Dave with Sam, winner of six open sheepdog trials on six consecutive Saturdays in the 1970s.

Right: Keeping a tradition alive. Dave shearing sheep by hand. He misses the days when neighbours came from all over the district to help with the clipping.

Below Right: Dave with two of his most successful dogs in the 1980s: Craig (left) and Gael.

Left: She's only nine weeks old, but Meg seems to be winning the approval of her new owner, Dave.

Right: The very picture of alertness: Meg at six months, eager to start work.

Below: Scott Smith with Meg's mother Jess and her litter of eight puppies. 'At five, Jess is in the prime of her life,' says Scott. 'She's a good mother, and she's made a great job of rearing the pups.'

Above: Blindburn in the grip of winter. Although storms aren't as severe as they used to be, the farm gets its fair share of snow.

Below: The isolated settlement of Makendon, pictured against the chequered landscape typical of the rolling Cheviot Hills. The last farm in the Upper Coquet valley, Makendon is now part of Blindburn.

feet all take their toll and, while medicines are available to treat various conditions, as ever, prevention is better than cure.

It's late spring at Linshiels and Dave has constructed a temporary sheep-handling pen in the corner of a field where ewes and lambs are kept. Cleverly designed to make use of the field's existing features, the pen utilises a wire-netting fence on one side and has a metal hurdle lashed to the side of a tractor on the other. Hurdles at either end serve as gates. This ingenious construction saves having to drive ewes and lambs a mile down the road to the main set of pens. They can be looked after on the spot, while remaining with their mothers.

The pen is just wide enough for a man to walk through the sheep, treating the lambs as he goes. This is what Robert MacKay, who works at the Carruthers' other farm, The Dunns, is doing. He's come to give Dave a hand. 'It takes two to do the job properly,' Dave explains. 'One to hold them in the pen and one to dose them.' The drug being applied to the lambs, from a dosing gun replenished by a pack on the shepherd's back, is a product aimed at eliminating ticks. A dab of the insecticide on the back of the neck is enough to treat the animal.

'We get ticks here bad in the spring,' Dave says. 'Horrible little creatures. They're blood-sucking parasites that stick to the skin, and they grow to the size of your little finger nail before they drop off. When one drops off there's usually half a dozen still there. They're awful hard to shift. They literally torture the lambs, biting away at them. They just about devour them.'

Ticks are the cause of a disease called 'louping ill' in sheep and battles have been waged against them for many years. Regular and controlled heather burning helped to reduce tick populations, but the amount of heather burned by farmers and shepherds has reduced in recent times. Flockmasters traditionally controlled ticks by dipping ewes shortly before lambing and lambs shortly after birth. But it's laborious and stressful to dip heavily pregnant ewes and now pyrethroid pour-on preparations, such as the one being applied to the lambs at Linshiels, are widely used instead.

For centuries, the curious practice of 'salving' or greasing was carried out with the aim of protecting sheep from the irritating attentions of ticks, lice and keds. Sheep were gathered into pens at a farm and lifted, one by one, onto a wooden trestle. Sheddings (partings in the wool) were made in a specific sequence at intervals of about an inch and a glutinous greasy mixture rubbed into the skin. The contents varied. A popular choice was Stockholm tar, thinned down by adding hot butter. Other recipes included whale oil, Brown George (old fat and oil from fleeces) and butter milk, which apparently helped it to spread better.

Salving, or 'sorving' as it was pronounced in some areas, was done in October and finished by tupping time. In 1299 an entry in the accounts at Bolton Abbey in Yorkshire lists 'oil and tallow to be used for salving the sheep £4.10s.' In 1794 the General View of Agriculture mentions that 1 gallon of tar and 17 pounds of butter would salve 21 to 30 sheep. The whole procedure was extremely labour-intensive and it took a shepherd 50 to 60 minutes to salve one sheep. Records from a Yorkshire farm refer to salving 600 sheep in four lots: ewes, hoggs, wethers and aged. An astonishing 410 man-hours were spent salving 510 sheep.

As well as supposedly killing parasites and preventing scab it was held that the salve also gave protection against the severe winter weather. There is no scientific basis to any of the claims made for the practice, yet it continued until compulsory dipping came into force in 1905.

Over the last century, the practice of dipping sheep has had a chequered history. Products have been developed which, while successful in controlling external parasites, have had worrying side-effects. In the mid-1960s sheep dips containing the pesticides aldrin and dieldrin were banned in Britain after it was discovered that they were having a harmful effect on wildlife. In the 1980s, farmers began using sheep dips containing organophosphate chemicals (OPs) after being compelled by the government to dip their sheep twice a year against scab. But there was anxiety over the long-term effect of OPs on members of the farming community after they began to visit their doctors complaining of headaches, depression, runny noses, and aching limbs – which they claimed only came on after dipping their sheep. In 1991 the compulsory dipping order was lifted.

In recent years the focus has once again been on the dangers posed by sheep dips to the environment. So strong are the chemicals contained in some dips that the smallest amount can have a devastating effect on aquatic life. The strict rules surrounding the siting of dipping baths and the disposal of the dip itself are forcing many farmers to look for alternatives. There has been a trend for those with smaller flocks to hire contractors with mobile dipping systems who come onto the farm, dip the sheep and dispose of the dip in a safe way, all as part of the service.

∾

Border Collies

Border Collies are the unsung heroes of British agriculture. Anyone who has watched them bringing a flock of stubborn Herdwick sheep down from the lofty peaks and hidden gullies of the Lake District, will know how accomplished they are. The job would be virtually impossible without a pack of these intelligent, hardworking dogs.

Developed by shepherds in the North of England and the Borders of Scotland over the last 150 years, the Collie breed of herding dog is renowned for its ability to muster sheep from the most inaccessible of spots and move them in a controlled, patient manner to where they're supposed to go.

So what's their history and where does the name Collie come from?

Anyone researching the origins of the Border Collie on the Internet could be forgiven for thinking that, like an inexperienced competitor at a sheepdog trial, they've taken the wrong direction round the course. For some strange reason, if you type in the name of the greatest sheepdog of all time in your search engine, you end up in the world of exotic substances. For the father of the modern collie was called Old Hemp. Not that he had anything to do with marijuana, of course, Hemp was just a monicker that appealed to his master. Like all sheepdog names, it's short and sweet. No point in having a long name to be blurted out repeatedly when a dog is being trained, or when it's working half a mile away from you on the windswept fells.

In his own particular world, Old Hemp was a one-off. Bred by Adam Telfer, of Cambo in Northumberland, he was born in 1894 and, in the words of one writer, 'blazed a path like a meteor across the sky'. Black and white with a long straight coat and semi-erect ears, Old Hemp stood 21 inches tall and weighed about 45 lbs. He started sheepdog trials at the tender age of one and never came anywhere but first. He had a remarkable ability to read sheep and finished every trials course without any apparent difficulty.

Reticent Scots, not normally given to fulsome praise, described him as 'bluidy marvellous'.

Old Hemp was a classic example of inspired breeding – coupled with a touch of luck. His father, Roy, was acknowledged to be a nice dog but he didn't have a special talent for herding sheep. His mother, Meg, however, was such an intense worker she was supposed to have developed the ability to hypnotise herself instead of the sheep. Somehow the combination worked. Hemp inherited all the good traits of his parents without being hampered by any of their faults.

Hemp was one of the greatest stud dogs in the history of Border Collies. In eight short years, in between his exploits on the trials front, he fathered more than 200 dogs and an unknown number of bitches. He must have been exhausted! Many of his progeny became successful trial dogs and in their turn bred more outstanding collies. It's claimed that you can trace the DNA of almost every Border Collie in the world back to Hemp. When he died in 1901, he had certainly left his mark.

Where does the name 'Collie' originate? A number of conflicting explanations have been put forward. There's speculation that it may have come from the word *kuli* in German, which is pronounced the same way as the term 'coolie', or worker. The dogs' immense appetite for work might seem to reinforce this theory. And in fact, there is a breed of dog called *Ald Deutscher Kuli* which is used for herding sheep. There is, however, a second possible source for the term. 'Collie' is an old Celtic word for anything useful, and Collie dogs have certainly proved their usefulness over the centuries. A third suggestion is that the word has something to do with the dogs' coat colour and that earlier spellings of the name – 'coly' or 'colley' or 'coalie' meaning black –

may stem from that. Or did it in fact refer to the colour of the sheep? They were predominantly black, and it could be the case that 'Collie' dogs were those which herded black sheep.

As I mentioned in a previous chapter, it's difficult to pinpoint the exact time when the interdependence between man and dog first began. Early nomadic tribes used the hunting instincts of the wild dogs they tamed to the mutual benefit of both species. Dogs would spot their prey, as they still do today, and master and animal would stalk and kill it to provide food for both. Later, when tribes began to settle, the dog became a useful tool in the early farmer's increasingly domesticated world.

The Romans were almost certainly the first to classify dogs into categories of hunting, guarding and shepherd's work. When the Romans invaded Britain in 55 BC, they brought along their dogs to assist with the control of their livestock. These black, tan and white dogs were large and heavy-boned, with a likeness to today's Bernese Mountain Dog or Rottweiler. As the Romans settled in this country and adapted to the climate, so did their dogs. They established themselves as having an important part to play in the care and protection of farmed animals. In AD 116 there's a record of an author named Marcus Terentius Varro, who is credited with having written many works on pastoral matters, including one on the care and training of the shepherd's dog.

As the Roman Empire began to crumble, the Vikings invaded the British islands, bringing with them the Spitz-type dogs they used for herding. These dogs must have eventually been crossed with the descendants of Roman herding dogs, reducing their size but probably increasing their agility. This change could have been an advantage in the hills of Wales and rocky highlands of Scotland.

One of the earliest written references to the appearance of herding dogs comes from the Welsh writer Hywel Dda in 943. He described a black sheepdog ushering a flock of sheep out to graze in the hills and coming home with them in the evening. This is a daily activity which, to some extent, still exists today in many hill farming areas. Five centuries later, other factors were at play in the continued development of the sheepdog to a more agile, less bulky animal. *English Dogges*, written in 1576 by Johannes Caius, contains a description of the breed which could easily be applied to our modern-day working collie:

> Our shepherd's dogge is not huge, vaste or bigge, but of indifferent stature and growth, because it hath not to deale with the blood thirsty wolfe, sythence there be none in England, which happy and fortunate benefite is to be ascribed to the puissant Prince Edgar. This dogge, either at the hearing of his master's voice or at the shrill hissing, bringeth the wandering wethers and straying sheep into the self same place where his master's will and wish is to have them, whereby the shepherd reapeth this benefite, namely that with little labour nor toyle or moving of his feete he may rule and guide his flock, according to his own desire.

Protecting flocks from marauding packs of wolves had been, until the end of the 16th century, an essential part of sheepdogs' lives. But when wolves were wiped out in Britain, the dogs' role as guardians diminished and their ability to gather and move large groups of sheep came very much to the fore. Before the days of railways and motor transport sheep had to be driven long distances to market, and without a handful of willing dogs to catch strays and keep the flock moving, those long droves would not have been feasible. Indeed, it may have been the drovers who marshalled big bunches of sheep through the English lanes of the 17th and 18th centuries who were responsible for the spread of the Collie dog. They liked dogs who didn't rush sheep, a quality recognised in the *Shepherds' Sure Guide* of 1749 where this rather matter-of-fact observation was made: 'A lame shepherd and a lazy dog are the best attendants on a flock of sheep because they do not over-drive or worry them.'

By the end of the 18th century packs of ill-disciplined dogs were roaming the streets of many towns and cities, prompting fears that they would cause rabies to spread. In an attempt to reduce numbers, a Dog Tax was introduced in 1796 and dogs which didn't have licences were destroyed. The measure may have had its desired effect in terms of clearing the streets of strays, but few realised what a severe impact it would have on shepherds and their families. The tax was eight shillings (about 40p) per animal, so a shepherd with four dogs faced an annual fee of one pound, twelve shillings (£1.60). That was a lot of money for impecunious shepherds to find. After representations to the Chancellor of the Exchequer by John Grey, of Dilston, near Corbridge in Northumberland, a wealthy landowner and leading figure in farming circles at the beginning of the 19th century, shepherds' dogs were made exempt in 1828. Grey's daughter, Josephine Butler, the social reformer, recorded in a memoir of her father that 'the general public do not know to this day what a boon to a considerable class of daily labourers was the removal of this tax.'

What most people hadn't grasped, she went on to say, was that one working dog was often not enough to gather sheep off a large area of moorland. As is still the case, at least two, or possibly three, would be required. In addition, a shepherd probably also needed a young Collie or two, who would serve their apprenticeships before replacing the older dogs. 'As the earnings of a shepherd are small and the maintenance of a dog is equal to that of a child among porridge-eating races the additional burden of a tax of up to 32 shillings was felt to be a great injustice.'

To appreciate the difference made by this change in the law in one county alone, the number of dog licence exemptions issued in Westmorland (now the southern part of Cumbria) in 1910 was 4,386, which was a far bigger figure than that for licences: 3,901.

As the 19th century progressed improvements in the Collie breed continued. Frank Garnett's account of farming in Westmorland between 1800 and 1900 shows a dramatic change: 'In the first decades of the 1800s no such dog as a Collie was mentioned and sheepdogs were selected from mongrels which showed the most appetite for herding. In later years the breed developed, dividing into two branches, the smooth- and the rough-coated. Many of these sheepdogs are large, upstanding smooth-coated animals, often wall-eyed, black or black-and-white in colouring. Others are rough or broken-coated, best described as "curs" with the highest sense of appreciation attached to the name.'

> The breeding of both varieties for generations has been by selection so as to emphasise a spirit of determination and sagacity to control sheep. A good dog requires these two points especially well-developed, together with a strong constitution and an ability to combat the waywardness and cunning of sheep on their own fellsides.

Keeping track of Border Collies' ancestry has become simpler since 1949 when the International Sheep Dog Society began to publish its early stud books, in which dogs' pedigrees had been traced back to the early 1900s. Today the pedigrees of some 6,000 pups continue to be registered each year, and in 2001 the society passed a milestone when it registered its 250,000th dog.

The modern father of the breed is a dog called Wiston Cap. Like Old Hemp, he had a huge influence and there are few Border Collies whose bloodlines cannot be traced back to him. He was International Sheepdog Trials Champion in 1965, when he was less than two years old, and he became the most popular stud dog in the breed's history. Wiston Cap was owned by John Richardson, of Peebles, who was known as 'Jock' to his friends. As a young man Jock had become fascinated with Border Collies and, like many shepherds, he would take his dogs out for further training after his day's work. Even on winter nights he continued to train them, working by moonlight if he had to. He had a calm manner, whistling commands through his fingers rather than using a plastic whistle, and he treated all his dogs alike, whether they were champions or also-rans.

Jock was a dedicated student of sheepdog breeding and in 1963 he bought a pup out of WS Heatherington's Fly, sired by his own Cap. The new arrival, Wiston Cap, came to Jock at six weeks old, and would lie on his master's coat watching him while the house cow was being milked. He was responsive to his master's every move. Jock claimed that Wiston Cap had only to be taught a thing once to remember it forever and he would lie in bed at night wondering what he could teach the dog next.

Wiston Cap possessed the classic Border Collie markings of white ruff and stockings on a black body, prick ears and white blaze, and his crouching style so epitomised the working collie that his image became the symbol of the International Sheep Dog Society. He went on to sire three Supreme International Champions and was grandsire of four more. Any offspring, known as 'Wiston Cappers' to sheepdog people, are always the focus of attention. Yet through all these triumphs, Jock remained completely unaffected. His trials dogs worked daily among the rocky outcrops, foaming burns and steep slopes of Scottish hill farms; none was kept purely for competition.

Jock Richardson died in 2000 at the age of 73. But the reputation of his dog remains as strong as ever. Staff at the International Sheepdog Society know Wiston Cap's registration number (31154) by heart, and are reputed never to file his card – because it's always in use.

Border Collie breeders buy and sell a lot of dogs privately, as do breeders of other kinds of dogs. But Collies are also sold on the open market – for prices which certainly raise a few eyebrows. One company which does this is Craven Cattle Marts. Three times a year they hold sheepdog auction sales at their mart at Skipton in North Yorkshire. The sales have one traditional feature: all the dogs are sold in guineas (£1.05), just as pedigree farm animals have always been sold. As a measure of their popularity, the sales attract more than 2,000 onlookers, among them many of Britain's sheepdog handlers, who are curious to know how much the dogs they work day-in day-out are fetching when they come under the hammer.

Unbroken dogs are displayed in a large pen, in the centre of which is a small pen with a handful of sheep in it. This gives a young dog the chance to show 'eye' as it circles the sheep in their pen, but it doesn't allow it to get too close to the sheep and make them anxious. Trained dogs, on the other hand, are given three minutes to display their talents herding a few sheep in a grassy amphitheatre as auctioneer Jeremy Eaton reads out their pedigree and invites bids. Purchasing a sheepdog on this sort of evidence may be a big risk to take but it doesn't seem to deter the buyers. In 2003, John Bell, from Howdon near Goole on Humberside, set a new British record when he sold a Collie bitch at Skipton for 3,150 guineas. At the same auction, he also sold Collies for 2,250 and 1,900 guineas. Both were bitches. On a day when a total of 60 dogs were on offer, trained animals averaged 1,200 guineas, unbroken dogs 500 guineas and pups 120 guineas.

John has had an interesting life. He kept sheepdogs and took part in trials as a teenager, but then gave it up to breed horses. Now 73, he finds horses too much to handle and has reverted to his first love. He breeds some dogs and buys in others, and at any one time has 20 or more at various stages of being trained. He has enough land on his smallholding to run nursery trials (for young dogs) at different times during the year.

John says none of the people who bought his top sheepdogs at Skipton bought them 'blind'. All had been to his home to see what they looked like first. 'We start training them at nine to ten months,' he says. 'Some people say that's too young but it works for me. Every dog is different and they all require individual attention.'

'Prices are definitely going up and demand is strong,' says Jeremy Eaton. 'Our May sale is popular with people who want a young dog to break in during the long summer evenings in preparation for tupping time in the autumn, and with an eye on nursery sheepdog trials the next year.'

∾

The Pup

'What are you going to call her?' Mona asks her husband as he's leaving the house.

'I don't really know,' Dave says. 'What do you think?'

After pausing to reflect, Mona says: 'I like the name Meg.'

Dave turns to his granddaughter Natalie. 'What about you, Natalie?'

'I like Meg too,' she says.

'Then Meg it is.'

Dave is about to leave on an special mission. He's going to pick a Border Collie pup from a litter being reared on a farm 40 miles away. As always, there's a sense of expectancy. Will there be a pup which comes up to his exacting standards? At least he's got over the first hurdle: the pup has a name – even though he hasn't bought it yet.

Natalie's come to stay with her grandparents for a few days. She loves being in the country, surrounded by sheep and sheepdogs. And the chance to go and help her granddad select the latest addition to his collection of dogs is too good to miss.

Dave and Natalie climb into his 4 x 4 and, waving to Mona, they set off on their journey. It's late spring and the Northumberland countryside is bursting with new growth. Old folks say that may (hawthorn blossom) brings bad luck if you take it into the house, but who would want to? It looks so beautiful where it is, cloaking the hedges with a magnificent white mantle. The strong, musky perfume of the flowers drifts into the car through the open windows.

Dave's 'farming the land' on both sides of the road as it wends through Netherton and Whittingham on the way to Alnwick and the coast. Farming folk are unfailingly curious about what's going on 'ower the dyke' and as they drive along with their eyes on the road ahead they're absorbing information about what's happening in the fields – and making mental notes which can be exchanged later over a pint at the pub or at the auction mart. They'll spot the flock of woodpigeons which – despite the presence of a gaudily-dressed scarecrow – is decimating a field of young oilseed rape plants; they'll secretly note the kinks left by a ploughman in an otherwise straight furrow; and they'll remark to themselves how the dry weather is reducing the amount of grass available for dairy cows at turn-out time. Nothing will escape their attention. But it means that having land next to a country road can make a farmer feel slightly exposed. It's a very public place to earn a living.

As they travel east, Dave chats to Natalie. For someone who can sometimes seem a little gruff, he is easy with his granddaughter. Both are wondering what sort of dogs they'll find at their destination.

The farm, located on the western edge of the fishing village of Seahouses, consists of a four-square farmhouse and a neat range of stone outbuildings roofed with red tiles. The property dates back more than 150 years. Its stables, water trough and hayloft are a relic of the days when Clydesdale horses lumbered through the farmyard on their way to working in the fields.

The farmer, Scott Smith, has been running the farm for almost half a century. Slim, erect, he was a stylish opening bat for the local cricket team for many years, and only declared his own innings when foot and mouth disease put paid to village cricket when it swept the country in 2001. Reviving an interest of his earlier life, he now breeds Border Collies and has grown passionately interested in training them for sheepdog trials. It's not something he'd entirely lost touch with: he was heavily involved as an administrator when the English National Sheepdog Trials were held in the area in 1977. But now he'd probably admit it: he's hooked – as a competitor.

The foot and mouth epidemic may have ended his career as a cricketer, but it was a defining moment in the re-awakening of his interest in sheepdogs, he says. 'At the time we had to have regular inspections from Defra vets, and because we couldn't always bring the sheep into the pens in the farmsteading, we had to check them in the fields. And of course that taught me quite a bit. It brought back skills from the dim and distant past, skills of handling and treating sheep in the field, and it showed me that perhaps these old skills could be brought back to the fore.'

In a sunlit corner the pups are suckling their mother Jess: eight black-and-white bundles of fur trying to draw one last drop from her almost dried-up teats. They are seven weeks old and nearly weaned. Scott, Dave and Natalie watch as the pups, refuelled with milk, start to scrap with one another, emitting a chorus of squeaks, growls and high-pitched yelps.

'Their mother's fed them well,' says Scott proudly.

'So have you, by the look of them,' Dave laughs.

'Well, they took to solid food quite early and they've never looked back,' Scott says. 'They've been regularly wormed to keep them healthy, and as you can see they're full of vigour.'

'You've quite a few to get homes for.'

'True, but I've had a lot of enquiries for them. They're mostly spoken for. They'll all be leaving each other in the next few days to start a new life in their various different homes, but who knows, they might meet up with one another some time in the future.'

'You'll be hoping they do meet up again at a sheepdog trial.'

'That's right. But even if they don't, they'll make good working dogs, I hope. After all, being a good working dog's the most important aspect of the Collie. It's not everyone who ends up at a trial.'

As they talk, Dave has been shrewdly assessing the pups playing at their feet. He says to Natalie, 'Pass that one up to me.'

Deftly, Natalie picks up a pup and hands it to her grandfather. The pup's a bitch, black and white with tan markings on her face and tan hair on the insides of her ears. Even at this young age she has an alertness about her, a quality emphasised by her pricked-up ears. She has that hard-to-define trait, 'character'. Dave holds her up in front of him, assessing her good points, looking for possible faults. Then, cradling her, he opens her mouth and peers down her throat. It's a test he learned from shepherds long ago.

'It's just to see what sort of colour they have in the mouth. It's just something I've always done. I don't like any white in their mouth.' Mercifully, the pup's mouth is as black as a coal hole.

Dave's got strong views on what an ideal Collie should look like. 'They shouldn't be too gaudy,' he says. 'Ideally, they should be black and white, with not too much white in the coat. A lot of folk like tan in their dogs, but if I had a choice I'd stick to black and white.'

Nevertheless, he seems pretty taken with the pup in his hands. 'Grand strong legs she's got,' he says. 'Good bone.'

He puts the pup back on the ground. Instead of racing off to join its siblings, it sits contentedly at Dave's feet. 'Which one should we choose?' Dave asks Natalie.

'That one with the pricky ears.'

'Well, that would be my choice too. It seems very calm. No signs of nerves. If they're nervous they're not much cop, all through their lives. No, this one's stayed beside me, so it must want to come home with us.'

Between them, they have found Meg.

Scott is pleased. 'She's a strong personality, that one. She lets the others know she's around. I wish you luck with her.'

The very fact that Meg is here at all is something of a triumph. 'This litter has an interesting history because it's hard to get Jess into pup in the first place,' Scott says. 'It's difficult to know for certain when she's in season and when she is, it's only for a short time. So when the moment comes, you've got to get on your bike, so to speak, and take her very quickly to the sire you have chosen for her.'

In this instance it meant travelling to Lonscale Farm near Keswick in Cumbria, the home of Derek Scrimgeour. For the last 19 years Derek has been tenant of the 12,500-acre (5,000-hectare) farm, which occupies one of the most spectacular settings in the Lake District. On one side looms the huge mass of Skiddaw, on the other, Blencathra frowns down.

Formerly a shepherd, Scots-born Derek has been fascinated by sheepdogs all his life, in spite of the fact that his first boyhood encounter with them wasn't a happy one. He was knocked down and attacked by a chained-up sheepdog, and for quite some time he was too terrified of dogs to go anywhere near them. It was only after receiving a pup as a present from his parents that he managed to overcome his fear of the animals.

As well as breeding and training dogs, Derek is author of *Talking Sheepdogs*, a new guide book on training Border Collies which lays much more emphasis on tone, volume and insistence of voice or whistle than on harsh physical pressure and threats.

'Your first step is to get rid of the thought that your dog is trying to defy you,' says Derek. 'It wants to work as your partner to help bring sheep under control.'

Derek's leading dog is an eight-year-old called Ben. 'He's a great all-round dog. He's suited me more than any dog I've ever worked with,' he says. Ben's best trial performance came in the 2002 international sheepdog trials in Ireland, where he came fifth. By mating Jess with Ben, Scott Smith is hoping for a litter of pups which reflect the best points of both parents. 'If they've been bred well they come truer to type when the time comes to train them. The good qualities of their ancestors hopefully come through,' says Derek.

But when it came to the pre-arranged mating day there was a small problem: the North of England weather. 'We got across to Keswick on this particular Sunday in February, and having gone that distance I usually stay over and make sure the bitch has a second service the following day,' Scott explains. 'But on this occasion it wasn't possible because we ran into a snow storm the next morning. It was a complete white-out and the only thing in my mind was to make my way home. It took eight hours to get back. So in fact Jess was served only once. But as you can see, it's turned out very successfully. Eight pups, and all doing well.'

There are five dogs and three bitches and, as the litter grew up, Scott began to make up his mind which pup he might keep for himself. 'It's difficult to decide at an early age which one of the litter to focus on as your favourite. It's only at the five to six weeks stage that they start to show character. You have your own likes and dislikes from that point. I had thought at the outset I'd be looking for a bitch this time to keep for myself and I've pretty well decided which one.'

That said, Scott is pleased with the male pups too. 'It's a very even litter and the mother has done them particularly well,' he says. 'At five years old Jess is in the prime of her breeding time. She's experienced, yet still quite young. It's her third litter and probably the best I've had from her.'

The timing of Jess's latest batch of pups was deliberate. 'April is a nice time of the year to have a litter of puppies,' Scott says. 'They've got the whole summer ahead of them. Like all young stock, sunshine's good for their development. And with longer days, they can stay outside later as well. We've had a great spell of dry weather this spring and I'm certain that's helped them to look so well too.'

One of the pups in the litter has quite distinctive markings. Apart from black ears, black patches over its eyes and a black spot on its tail, it's completely white. Physically it's perfect. But Border Collie breeders are split over the merits of such an animal. 'It wouldn't be my natural preference, a white dog,' admits Scott. 'But there's no reason to suppose that a white dog wouldn't turn out to be just as successful as a herding dog as any other Collie dog. It might be less successful, perhaps, as a trials animal, though. At home your sheep may get used to that particular dog, whatever colour it is. But when you take a white dog to someone else's farm, or to a trials field where the sheep don't know the dog, it does tend to spook them slightly and you can have a rather greater problem in controlling the sheep and keeping them calm. That's the fear the trial men have about white Collie dogs. And that's why they're not naturally their first choice.'

Nevertheless, white Border Collies do have some admirers.

They are popular with non-farming families, precisely because they look different. 'I never have any problem finding a home for a white dog,' Scott says.

Dave's got an open mind on the subject. 'I think it's true that sheep sometimes don't respond so readily to a white dog. They think, what's this white thing? Whereas a black dog, or a tan dog, they respond to them all right. All the same, I've had a white Collie bitch in the past and she was a good worker.'

After a cup of tea and the exchange of a few stories, it's time to set off on the journey home, with Meg taking pride of place – cuddled in Natalie's arms. She's left the place of her birth. What will life with her new owner, a shepherd, bring?

Within a month, Meg is showing some of the attributes of a grown-up sheepdog, as well as all the habits of a puppy. She's content to sit outside her kennel chewing an old stick. She barks at nothing in particular. She likes digging up the long-rooted docks growing beside the stone wall that shelters Dave's garden. But she's also aware of the other inhabitants of the smallholding.

Like many shepherds, Dave has a flock of hens. They're Brown Leghorns, an ancient breed of farmyard fowl with brilliantly-coloured feathers. While the hens appear generally nervous the two cockerels, as you might expect, have a rather jaunty air. Meg seems to see the hens as smaller versions of the sheep she will eventually learn to gather. Even at this early stage she is showing the beginnings of 'eye', her whole posture tense like a true Collie as she sizes up the birds and uses her staring pupils to exercise mental control over them. Then she becomes a puppy again, running after the hens in a demented way. Turning this untrained youngster into a dog which will heed its master and round up sheep will take time and patience.

Scott Smith says everyone has their own way of training dogs. 'There's no set method of doing it. You've got to try to look at each individual dog because they all have their own characteristics. Some dogs have very strong personalities, and you have to deal with that, whereas others are quite timid, although given time they will do a very good job indeed.'

'The principal objective for sheepdogs is herding sheep. It's a relatively small number which make the higher grade to the trial field. But trying to achieve that of course is very interesting. I enjoy training young dogs and bringing them on, and after that I sometimes let the more experienced handlers take them on from there. They can possibly see what further potential those young dogs might have.'

Dave's objective in training a sheepdog is simple: 'I don't keep them unless they go to the top,' he says. 'They have to make the grade. They have to win, really, to stay with me. If they don't win they don't stay. They go away to different people. Other handlers get them, and they're quite pleased with them. But for me the sole object of getting a pup is to win. That's what I'm trying to do.

'I don't keep a great lot of dogs. Nowadays I just keep one pup at a time and give it a fair chance. If you get two or three pups they never get a decent chance, because when you're working with one the other ones aren't getting enough exercise or work with stock. It's not fair to the dog. You just want to concentrate on one at a time.'

By the time she reaches five months, Meg is eager to impress her personality on sheep. When she's among them she shows no concern. 'She comes right up to them,' Dave says admiringly. 'That's a quality you don't often get in a young pup. They're usually lying a long way back, showing a lot of "eye" but not budging. You have to coax them to come up to the sheep. This one, you have to stop her.'

He takes another dog, Nap, with him when the pup is working with sheep in these early months of her life. Nap keeps the sheep at close quarters, making sure they don't run away from Meg. 'She can be a bit silly,' Dave says. 'She needs a bit of steadying up at times. But she's "shaping" on sheep, by which I mean she's showing "eye" and going round the sheep, keeping them to me.'

With her long legs and big feet, Meg will grow into a good-size bitch. 'She'll stand a lot of running,' Dave says. 'She's short-coupled, and a short-coupled dog is like a short-coupled racehorse, it has more stamina and lasts longer.'

By the time she's nine months old, Meg is looking every inch the working sheepdog. Some of her impulsive urges still surface, but she's becoming more and more composed. 'She is head-strong,' Dave admits, 'and she's taken more handling than I would have liked. But she'll make the grade. I'm pleased with her. She's got good balance on her sheep. She doesn't jump or flap about, she stays locked on to them.'

Dave keeps some sheep in a field next to the church at Alwinton and Meg is being trained to herd them. Dave reckons she's got that hard-to-define collie quality, power. 'She's keen, and she's got plenty of power, just like the dog that fathered her, Derek Scrimgeour's Ben. I saw him run at the English national sheepdog trials and I liked him. That's why I suggested to Scott Smith that he should take his bitch to him. Power's built in; either a dog's got it or it hasn't. If it hasn't got power and concentration, the sheep will just chase it about. They can read a dog straight away and know whether it can move them – or whether they can just play with it.'

Dave insists that the secret to training a successful collie is to have a good dog to start with. 'A dog that will listen, a dog that will stop when it's told to.' How firm does a dog owner have to be? 'You have to be firm but fair,' Dave maintains. 'Pat them but don't pet them because it breaks their concentration.'

He teaches his dogs by using verbal commands at first: how to go out left – 'Come bye' – and right – 'Away to me' – stop and come on. Then he introduces them to the whistle. 'When they break away to whatever side you want them to go, you just give them a little toot on the whistle and they soon pick up the idea that they can be controlled by whistle as well as by voice commands.'

For Dave, the satisfaction comes from spotting a dog's potential and developing it. He's looking for a dog that has the knack of performing well in sheepdog trials at weekends, together with the ability to handle sheep capably on its own farm. 'There's a strong sense of competition at the trials,' he says, 'especially when you're from Northumberland and you're competing in Scotland; there's a lot of friendly rivalry between us and the Scots. A lot of people think it's easy to go away and win a trial, but it isn't. You think you're good at home, but then you go away and compete against someone else, and you find out they're better!'

~

Sheep Bells

Anyone who has paused for a few minutes on their way through a mountainous region of Europe will have been charmed by the lilting sound of sheep bells echoing across a valley. The animals themselves are usually invisible as they graze beneath the trees, but the soft tinkling rises up through the air and reassures their owner that they haven't wandered too far. Sheep bells have died out in England, but until the 19th century they were still in widespread use. The main areas where they could be found were the southern counties, where large flocks were spread out over the rich downland pastures, and there are also records of them being used on the Pennines and the Welsh uplands. But they seemed to fade out the further north you came and few Scottish flocks are known to have used them.

By attaching bells to sheep, either by a leather collar or a small wooden yoke carved from gorse or thorn, shepherds were providing themselves with an early-warning system, like closed circuit television without the cameras. From the sound alone, they knew how their sheep were faring even if they were out of sight some way away. When the animals were peacefully grazing with their heads down the bells emitted a soft, chunking sound. When they were quietly looking for fresh grass to nibble or a pond to drink from the bells gave a rhythmic clunk-clunk-clunk noise. A small, short-lived peal probably meant they were shaking their heads to ward off flies. But when they were disturbed by the approach of strangers, or were threatened by a stray dog, the bells would jangle loudly and continuously as the sheep became restless and threatened to panic.

The sound of the bells was especially helpful to a shepherd after dark, in a fog or when thieves were on the prowl. Even today, sheep stealing still occurs in remote areas of the country, but it's not on the scale it was in the 19th century when it was almost endemic in sheep-farming areas, even those that were well-shepherded.

To us the sound may be evocative of a peaceful pastoral era, but not everyone enjoyed listening to sheep bells tinkling day and night. Villagers whose houses lay next to fields where sheep were grazing complained that the monotonous sound of their bells stopped them from getting their sleep. But shepherds loved the sound and openly confessed they 'missed the music' when the bells were removed at shearing time and the only sounds were the baa-ing of the ewes and the bleating of their lambs. In his book *A Shepherd's Life* the countryside writer WH Hudson suggests that the sound of the bells was, first and foremost, a companionable noise which lifted the spirits of shepherds working by themselves. One told Hudson: 'It is lonesome with the flock on the downs. More so in cold, wet weather when perhaps you don't see a soul all day – on some days not even at a distance, much less to speak to. The bells keep us from feeling it too much. They are company to us. We know what we have them for, and the more we have the better we like it.'

However, the bells belonged to the shepherd, and not to the owner of the flock he looked after, so on average the number of sheep which wore them was limited to about thirty. To be sure, shepherds would have liked to swell the sound of their orchestra of bells by having more, but their meagre wages did not allow for such extravagance. So they watched their flocks to see which sheep liked to be in the vanguard and fitted them with bells which could be heard at a great distance. Smaller, more musical bells were reserved for more cautious animals who preferred to stay close to the shepherd.

Bells came in a number of different styles. The cheaper – and more widespread – sorts were made of sheet metal, sometimes by a specialist bell-maker but more usually in the forge of the local blacksmith. One type was the 'clucket' or 'clucker' bell, which varied in size from three to six inches. The cluck-cluck sound it made could be heard a long way away. 'Here come the old cluckers,' the shepherds would say when they heard their sheep approaching. The other kind of bell was cast in bell-metal by bellfounders and was consequently more expensive. The most common was the 'cup' bell, which looked like an upturned cup. The bell-shaped 'latten' and the spherical 'crotal' were also popular: the sound came from a metal ball which rolled round inside the bell as the animal moved its head from side to side.

Sheep bells were still being cast at foundries in the Midlands in the early years of the 20th century, when there was still a demand from South Africa and South America. But bells which have survived in this country from the 17th and 18th centuries are now mostly to be found in museums of rural life.

7 Summer

~

Sheepdog Trials

Now he sends the dogs out round the sheep with calls of 'Gan Oot
  wide'
And whistles with a note so shrill the dog claps in his stride
'Come by here, Moss, lie doon a bit – or I'll stick your dusty hide'
That's the canny shepherd laddie of the hills.

Shepherds on farms hidden away in the hills may lead a lonely
life, but they like to get together whenever they can and they've
always shown a fierce desire to compete with one another. In
earlier times that applied to sheepdogs as much as to sheep.
Shepherds pitted their best dogs against their colleagues' at
informal sheep gathering events throughout the 19th century
before sheepdog trialling as a sport was properly formalised in
the 1870s.

It's generally accepted that the first so-called international
sheepdog trial was staged at Bala in North Wales on October 9,
1873. 'International' was rather a grand title since the only two
nations competing were Scotland and Wales, but it was a start.

Looking back, people wonder how the Scottish team got there. Did they take their dogs on the train? Were there any trains to Bala? Where did they stay? Whatever the answers, it was an occasion which attracted more than a passing amount of interest. Ten dogs and their owners competed before a healthy crowd of 300 onlookers. A contemporary account of the event describes how every dog had to herd 'three Welsh mountain sheep released from the arms of the sturdy Welshmen who had charge of that portion of the entertainment'. The contest had an interesting outcome, too. It was won by William Thompson with Tweed, a black and tan Border Collie of Scottish descent. Thompson was a Scot by birth but at that time he was working in Wales. Maybe being the one who didn't have to travel so far he was fresher for the fray. But it can't have pleased the Scottish entrants to have one of their own running for his adopted country of Wales, especially when he went on to beat the whole of the Scottish contingent!

In other parts of the United Kingdom national trials followed rapidly. Scotland held its first in 1874, and in 1876 England, not wanting to be outshone, put on its first national at Byrness, Northumberland. The winner was Walter Telfer from the nearby village of Cambo, brother of Adam Telfer, the man who bred the legendary collie Old Hemp.

In 1906 the International Sheep Dog Society was set up to 'stimulate interest in the shepherd and his calling' and to promote better management of stock by improving the shepherd's dog, because 'without good working dogs the job of the shepherd, both on the hills and in the lowlands, is well nigh impossible'. The society emphasises that these are still its objectives today.

An important step towards doing that, the society decided, was to have sheepdog trials run on a properly constituted basis. On August 30, 1906, the society held its first official international sheepdog trials at Gullane Hill in East Lothian in Scotland. First prize went to Robert Sandilands with Don. Although there were just 27 entries there was a great deal of interest in the traditionally-clad shepherds and their dogs, as the *Scottish Farmer* newspaper reported:

'It was a red letter day for the knights of the plaid and this they seemed to fully recognise. Many grey-bearded veterans were there, some to try their skills, and others to look upon the prowess of their brethren. There was no envy or jealousy evinced, each new arrival being greeted in the most cordial manner. When the great masters of the sheepdog world made their appearance there could be seen on the faces of the younger and less tried men a look of pride that their profession could boast such heroes.'

Sheepdog trials have continued under the jurisdiction of the ISDS to this day. They provide a way to compare dogs of different skills. The farm may be where a dog is put through its paces in ordinary working conditions day after day, but it's on the trials field, in front of a knowledgeable audience, that a dog reveals its true ability and the skill of the dog handler is properly tested.

A beautiful day in July sees Dave Baxter at Flotterton Hall Farm near Hepple, a few miles down the Coquet Valley from the hill farm where he works. The sheepdog trial at Flotterton is one of 27 held each year by the Northumberland Sheepdog Trials League between the end of May, when lambing time is coming to an end, and the beginning of October, when shepherds are busy preparing for the autumn lamb sales. It's organised by David Ogilvie, one of the shepherds at Flotterton, with the blessing of the Walton family who run the farm.

The setting for the trial is perfect. At the lower end of the site, wetlands created by gravel extraction are a haven for waterfowl. Skeins of wild geese in V-formation swoop low over the valley and mallard chatter noisily. In the distance, shimmering in the haze, the heather-covered ridge of the Simonside Hills rises above the dark shadow of a forest.

A row of cars, 4 x 4s and pick-ups and assorted dog trailers line the southern part of the field with one vehicle standing out by itself – it belongs to the judge, Mike Northwood. He has the difficult task of picking the six best competitors. It's an honour to be invited to officiate at a sheepdog trial, but it can be an isolating experience. The late Matt Mundell, an accomplished writer on sheepdogs and shepherds, once wrote: 'A trials judge is a man who cheerily starts the day with parents, relatives, friends, opinions, a Christian name, sanity, pride and a profound knowledge – and finishes the job bereft of the lot.'

Four hundred yards away, at the top of the gently-sloping field, galvanised metal hurdles are arranged in a series of pens holding a couple of hundred sheep. They will be released as each competitor steps forward to the handler's post, dog at heel, poised to begin his run.

For the first few hours of the day Dave's role is to let sheep out of the pens. As a close friend of the organiser, he's willingly volunteered for the task – at a local trial like this it's all hands to the pump. For each competitor, four sheep are released. They're Mule gimmers, once-shorn female sheep created by using Bluefaced Leicester rams on Swaledale or Blackface ewes. The North of England is famous for its Mule ewe lambs, which are bought in large numbers by sheep farmers from southern England and crossed with Suffolk sheep to produce lambs for the butcher.

There are about 30 competitors but most have brought two dogs with them so there will be 60 dogs running. If they last the course and negotiate every obstacle, it will take each dog about ten minutes. Even starting at eight o'clock, it's going to be a long day. The sun will be setting when the time comes to hand out the prizes.

Sheepdog handling was catapulted into the public's attention in 1976 after a BBC television producer, Philip Gilbert, stopped to watch a trial at Glanton Show in Northumberland while on holiday in the area. The intelligence of the dogs, the intense but comradely rivalry between the handlers and the tranquil beauty of the setting captured his imagination. He was convinced that the minority-interest rural pastime he had witnessed that wet Saturday afternoon could be transformed into a factual entertainment show with wide appeal. The outcome was *One Man and his Dog*. The first series consisted of seven half-hour programmes, which were an immediate hit. The BBC, surprised by its success, commissioned a further series and the number of people watching the programmes continued to grow. On Sunday evenings families from all sorts of backgrounds settled down in front of their television sets to marvel at shepherds' dogs showing off their skills.

One Man and his Dog became an institution. At its peak in 1981 it attracted an astonishing eight million viewers, the size of audience most broadcasters would die for now. It ran for 23 years and gave many people a glimpse of the countryside they would otherwise never have had. It also taught a lot of viewers the technical terms used in sheepdog trialling. But viewing fashions change and in 1999, with the audience down to 1.6 million, the BBC pulled the plug on the series.

The decision provoked a storm of protests from the programme's aficionados, many of whom accused the Beeb of walking away from its rural responsibilities. In what was seen as something of a peace offering the broadcaster came up with the idea of a Christmas special, a one-off programme without the location reports profiling individual handlers but featuring TV personalities and hosted by celebrity cook Clarissa Dickson-Wright. Some die-hard supporters of the programme in its original form say it's not to their taste, but the ratings have improved – and it continues to give the specialist world of sheep-dog handling an opportunity to bring the skills of dogs and handlers to a wider audience.

At Flotterton, not surprisingly, there's just a handful of spectators. Most of the people watching intently as proceedings unfold are competitors. But this is, after all, a local trial. National and International sheepdog trials still manage to attract big crowds.

The course is laid out over a grassy field with seemingly few undulations to deter a sheep or confuse a dog. At the top end, where the sheep are held, there's a minor road and participants can sometimes hear the sound of lorries trundling up the valley. On the left side of the course there's a small shelter belt of densely packed conifers. It doesn't look a difficult course to negotiate, but only time will tell. The aim, as most will know, is to collect four sheep and persuade them to follow a certain route round the course before being shut in a pen.

A ballot is drawn to decide when handlers will run their dogs, but it's a flexible arrangement. The course director will allow a handler to run a dog earlier in the day if the handler explains that he (or she) has to get back to the farm to work in the afternoon. The same applies to a handler who wants to go off to compete in another local trial. Likewise, someone who's decided to make a day of it and stay at a trial for the duration of the proceedings might agree to delay his run to let someone else get away. This generosity is frequently shown, despite the fact that when you run can have an effect on the result. Collies are never less than enthusiastic, but in the heat of the day even they can get distracted. On the other hand, there might be a breeze blowing first thing in the morning which makes it hard for a dog to hear commands. Sheep can vary tremendously too. Some are used to being worked with dogs, others aren't 'dog-broke'; they've just been herded by people on quad bikes and tend to be less biddable. Furthermore, some breeds are easier than others. Big sheep like Suffolks may need to be 'bossed' around the course, others like Swaledales may be more flighty and need kid-glove treatment. In addition to this, sheep, like dogs, can vary according to the time of day. Late in the afternoon, for instance, some sheep can be more of a handful. When they're the last in the pens, they're hungry and all their mates have gone, they're quite likely to go looking for them – at a gallop.

One of the most experienced competitors at Flotterton is Raymond MacPherson, a Scottish-born farmer who, before retiring a couple of years ago, spent 35 years as tenant of Tarn House, a farm which rises to 2,000 feet at Tindale Fell on the windswept Pennines near Brampton in Cumbria. Raised in the high country round Ben Nevis Raymond spent his early years working with his father, Andrew, who had started his farming life in the 1920s as a shepherd laddie droving sheep for 50p a week. 'Off the beaten track' was an exact description of the lonely hill farm where the MacPhersons lived in the 1950s. There was no access to it for vehicles, which meant an eight-mile walk to a point on the nearest road, where they left their car – something you could do in those days without worrying whether it would be there when you got back.

At weekends father and son, both sheepdog-mad, would leave the comfort of their farmhouse at 5 am and walk for two hours before bundling their dogs into the car and setting off for a local trial. 'You learned the hard way,' Raymond says. 'So too did your dogs.'

He eventually got his own farm in north Sutherland, a huge spread of nearly 20,000 acres sparsely populated by 600 North Country Cheviot ewes. 'It was a harsh introduction to farming on my own,' Raymond recalls. He couldn't afford staff, so he shepherded the place himself with the help of his dogs. 'I'd walk 20 miles a day to "look" the sheep,' he says.

He moved to Tarn House in 1965. The North Pennines can be inhospitable, but overall the Cumbrian countryside was preferable to the isolated wastes of Scotland's tip. The only drawback was that, as far as sheepdog trials were concerned, he was considered an Englishman. Not that it matters Raymond, now 71, has a record bettered by very few. His wins include the English National, the International (twice), the World Championship (twice) and television's *One Man And His Dog*. He says: 'I went to my first trial in 1939 and I remember it just like it was yesterday. I started competing in 1944 at the age of 11 and I won the very first trial I went to. Two weeks later I came second. It was a fine start, but you quickly learn that you can't always win. You need a lot of luck, as well as a good dog. Sometimes it's been tough but I've enjoyed every minute. If I had my life to live over again I wouldn't change anything.'

Sheepdog trialling has given Raymond an immensely full life and taken him all over the world. His first World Championship was won in America in 1973 and he has been back to the States 29 times as competitor and judge. The biggest change he's noticed has been the phenomenal increase in the number of women handling sheepdogs. At one American trial he judged early in 2004, women took the first eight places. They're prepared to travel great distances too. One woman flew with her dogs from Alaska to compete in a trial Raymond was judging in Texas. Moreover, comparatively few have agricultural backgrounds: the winner was a female librarian from New York.

Raymond isn't due to run his dog Jess yet, so as he watches one of the other handlers he's happy to describe how a dog should run, given the best of weather conditions and a co-operative 'packet' of sheep.

The first stage is the 'outrun'. The four sheep are released from pens 400 yards away and it helps immensely if the competing dog can catch sight of them before it sets off to gather them. 'A dog's outrun should be pear-shaped. Not too wide at the start,' says Raymond.

A dog is allowed to run up either side of the course, left or right. It may have a natural preference, but the handler will sometimes overrule that and decide that one side is better than the other because of the course layout. Shortly before their turn, some handlers take a dog out of the car and set it up next to them on the side it's going to be run on. They then put the dog back in the car to think about it, before repeating the exercise to imprint on the animal which side it's going to make its outrun.

The outrun is followed by the 'lift', which involves approaching the four sheep and collecting them calmly together. 'The dog shouldn't stop short of the sheep at the top of the course, but should go round to the balance of the sheep,' says Raymond. 'They should be at 12 o'clock, but of course, being sheep, they're not always where you hope they will be.'

The 'fetch' is the next part of the trial. It's the job of bringing the sheep all the way down the course to the handler, who must remain at his station, a post driven into the ground not far from where the judge is positioned. 'The dog should lift them gently but with feeling and bring them down the field. There might be the odd wobble, but try and be as straight as possible. The handler has to be in line between the sheep and the dog, and they come always to him – straight. The pace has to be right too, just walking pace, not too fast. A lot of dogs can do it fairly well on their own if they're well-schooled and well-balanced, but they'll need commands at times. Some need commands all the time.'

After the lift comes the 'drive'. Dogs must bring the quartet of sheep round behind the handler's back and move them towards the first obstacle, a pair of gates four yards apart which are positioned 150 to 200 yards away on the right of the course. 'It's not always possible when you're working with animals', Raymond says, 'but try to be as perfect as you can. Walk the sheep in a straight line, calmly, and ease them through the gates as gently as possible.'

The first leg of the drive is followed by the 'cross drive'. For this part of the trial the sheep have to be turned and steered across the centre of the course and between two more gates, also four yards apart. 'Your dog has to be in good command at all times,' Raymond says, 'and this obstacle can be awkward, difficult to judge. Just keep your cool. For the dog to be calm, the handler has to be calm.'

The challenge is to keep the sheep moving as they progress through the three legs of the drive. Make them go a bit faster than they want to go, is the usual advice. If they're used to travelling at five miles an hour make them go at six.

The last section of the drive involves bringing the sheep back towards the handler in preparation for the 'pen'. This is often the trickiest moment of all. Trying to coax four sheep into a small pen made of hurdles in the middle of a field takes a great deal of skilled co-operation between dog and master. Instinct warns the sheep not to become trapped in a small confined space; at the same time, too much pressure from the dog will set the sheep on edge. One will often make a bid for freedom, only to be rounded up and brought back to join the group. Then there will be a stand-off, with the stubborn sheep refusing to budge, and the dog not giving way either. And all the time the clock is ticking: handlers are given a set time to complete the course (at the Flotterton trial it's actually 11 minutes) and they're penalised if they take too long. Some actually carry their own stop-watch to give them an idea of how much time is left.

For this section of the trial the handler is allowed to leave his station and approach the pen. As he grips the six-foot rope holding the gate, knowing it must slap shut to complete this stage of the run, he has to stop himself from becoming nervous, as all eyes are turned on him and his dog. Raymond makes the point that it's the first time the sheep have come close to the handler, so it's up to him to calm them down and make it easier for everyone. 'Take your time and don't be in too big a hurry,' he says. 'Too hurried and you'll frighten the sheep and fluster your dog. Too laid-back, and you'll get nowhere. You must study the sheep, and your dog must be steady: tight on the sheep but not too tight. A properly handled dog can come in to the sheep when commanded and stay off when commanded. The gentle way is the best way at the pen – if you can manage it.'

One piece of advice handlers are often given is that sheep don't like to look at two things at the same time, so a dog should be still when his handler is moving and when the dog is moving his master should remain motionless.

The final part of the trial is the 'shed', which entails splitting the four sheep into two pairs. It looks the easiest of all the tests, but it can be as problematical as the rest. The last two sheep out of the pen must be the ones to be 'shed' from the others. This is a test of a dog's bravery, as it has to confront the rear two sheep's heads as it splits the first two off. Sometimes handler and dog are so relieved to have penned the sheep that they relax and consequently take too long over the shed. Sometimes the sheep are particularly bloody-minded by this stage of the proceedings and are determined to show it. To them, there's safety in numbers; no group of sheep wants to be divided in two. Shepherd and dog just have to choose their moment. A gap will open up between the sheep and the dog can dart through and separate them.

All the tasks set by the trials course have practical uses and apply to normal working conditions on the farm. A dog will be asked to run wide and collect a flock of sheep and bring them near to the shepherd, as happens in the outrun, lift and drive. It will be asked to get sheep into pens, and will be told to split off a ewe or a ewe with lambs. Shepherds who go to trials assert that they get more from their dogs because they are taught with trials, as well as day-to-day farm work, in mind. 'Top men and top dogs can gather sheep on any hill, on any field and in any situation,' says Raymond Macpherson. 'It's much easier for a top-class dog handler to gather his sheep rather than someone who doesn't run. Shepherds who don't go to trials don't train their dogs to go that extra bit. Sheep can get into hollows, hidden corners and streams and you can guide your dog to get them out, if it's well trained. A dog that's not so determined will miss them.'

At a local trial like Flotterton the scoring system goes like this. Each competitor starts off with 100 points and has points deducted for mistakes at every stage. The outrun is worth 20 points, the lift ten, the fetch 20, the drive 30 (ten for each leg), the pen ten and the shed ten. The points count even if a handler has run out of time.

While handlers are anxious to win a trial, coming in the first six is also a worthwhile achievement because it counts towards qualification to take part in National trials. Under this scheme, winners of local trials get six points, second five, third four and so on. If you win three local trials you automatically qualify to run in the National. These are held in England, Scotland, Wales and Ireland (including the Isle of Man) each year, attracting up to 200 dogs in each and to qualify a dog must have accumulated at least 13 points from local trials.

The top 15 dogs at the English, Welsh, Irish and Scottish Nationals comprise the teams which compete at the International. At this event, the same size of course and number of sheep is used for the qualifying trial, which is run over the first two days. But on the third and final day the course is lengthened to 700 yards, with a double 'lift', and a total of 20 sheep are piloted round the course. This is one of the greatest tests a sheepdog can be put through and worthy is the winner who boasts the title of 'supreme champion'.

In September 2002 the first multi-nation World Sheepdog Trial was held by the ISDS at Bala in Gwynned, the same location as the 1873 trial. With 122 competitors from 13 nations, and 18,000 visitors, the event was deemed a big success. The final saw handlers from Germany, France, Norway and the Netherlands compete with handlers from England, Ireland, Scotland and Wales. The next World Sheepdog Trials are being planned for 2005 with teams attending from as far as the USA, Australia and New Zealand.

It's midday before it's Dave's turn to run his first dog. He strides to the post, his crook hooked over his right forearm. It's 50 years since he first went to a sheepdog trial as a young shepherd just starting his career. 'There were a lot of experienced old men at those trials. Some didn't want to know you, and some were quite helpful,' says Dave. 'If they could be bothered to talk to a young lad they could tell you a thing or two about sheepdogs. An old chap over the Border, Tom Watson, he taught me a great lot.' At the age of 18 Dave went to help with the lambing at a hill farm called Cottonshope, near Byrness in Northumberland. 'There was a shepherd there, Davie Rogerson, who had a vast knowledge of dogs and sheepdog trials. He told me everything he knew, particularly about the breeding of the dogs and how to train them. He had a lot of time for a young man. A really good chap, was Davie.'

In 1956 the International Sheepdog Trials were held at Ayr and Davie let Dave drive him there in his ancient car. 'It was an experience', Dave says. 'Travelling along in an old banger and listening to him talking about dogs as we drove across the country and looked at the farms with the autumn colours coming on. He was a great fellow to be with on your first trip to a big occasion like that.'

When Dave left Cottonshope the old shepherd gave him a bitch pup he had bred. 'I had her for years,' Dave recalls. 'That was the start of it, as far as sheepdogs and trialling was concerned. Then I got a dog called Sam. I bought him off a shepherd in Wooler. I can remember it clearly. We had white £5 notes as well as blue in those days. He was a chap who liked his money – don't we all? – and he looked at the note and looked at the pup. Then he grabbed the note and shoved the pup at me, and the deal was done.'

Before long, Dave was addicted to sheepdog trials. Every Saturday and Sunday throughout the summer he'd be off running his dogs. Sam turned out to be an inspired buy. He won his first trial when he was only nine months old, which is quite exceptional, and he continued to show a huge appetite for trials as he matured.

Dave swears that Sam could tell which day of the week it was. The dog certainly knew when it was Saturday. 'Any other day of the week he'd just wander around the place, staying calm. But on Saturdays he'd run outside and stand near the pickup, and then run into the kitchen and stand next to my stick. He knew it was the day to go to the trials. And in the car he'd sit behind me, chin resting on the back of my seat, watching. He seemed to know where we were going.'

Dave recalls a trial at Heddon-on-the-Wall in Northumberland where one of the sheep in Sam's 'packet' had a sore udder which was making her very obstinate. The last place she wanted to be was on a field being chivvied by a dog and she let Sam know what she felt by stamping her feet in a show of aggression. 'She shouldn't have been among the sheep being used at the trials,' Dave says.

Calmly but firmly, Sam backed the ewe all the way down the course from the release pen to the post where Dave was issuing commands. It was an impressive piece of handling.

One Saturday the pair established something of a record. They set off at daybreak for Canonbie in Dumfriesshire, where Sam ran in the local trial. Dave then drove back to Northumberland where he competed in four more trials, returning home at dusk exhausted. 'Mind, I didn't have a very good car in those days,' he smiles, 'and the engine was red hot when we got home!'

Dave makes it clear that it wasn't just for financial reward that he took part in so many trials. 'It was the competing that counted – and the winning. In 1965 that dog Sam won six trials six Saturdays running.' Nevertheless, prize money back in the 1950s and 1960s was surprisingly good. The winner of a trial could receive as much as £10, which for anyone on a shepherd's wage was certainly worth having. Dave may have travelled more than 150 miles in his desire to compete at as many trials as possible, but it was worth it. 'Yes, on that particular day I won a few prizes,' he grins, 'but it was just a pleasure, running Sam. He just loved to perform – and he always gave you everything he had.'

Many other dogs which Dave bred and used in trials made their mark over the years, among them Betty, Don, Craig and Gael, a bitch that won the Northumberland Sheepdog Trials League six times in the 1980s.

Today, it's the turn of Nap, a four-year-old dog. On his master's whispered command Nap sets off on his outrun. It's the requisite pear shape and within a minute he's closing in on his four sheep when, unaccountably, he stops and lies down. 'He shouldn't have done that, ' says Dave, 'but sometimes that's the kind of thing a dog will do and you just have to get on with it.' He sends a piercing whistle and instantly Nap's up and starting to bring the sheep straight down the field at a steady pace, yet under perfect control. The 'fetch' gains almost maximum points. 'Take time, lad!' Dave urges as Nap neatly turns the sheep behind his master and back up the course towards the first drive gates. Just as they seem as though they're going to saunter aimlessly past the gates the sheep are neatly guided through them by Nap, who makes a tidy job of the cross drive before making an error which will cost him dear. He pushes the sheep through the second pair of gates and then, for no apparent reason, allows them to wander back through the gates again.

'He's normally a good listener,' Dave says, 'but there were times on the course when he just didn't seem to hear right. When the wind gets up the sounds of the whistle and your commands seem to echo from the little wood at the side, and that may have thrown him. But it's the same for everybody. He should have listened, but he didn't. And that's lost us a whole heap of points.'

At the pen, Nap and Dave illustrate exactly how good some man-and-dog combinations can be. The sheep are showing signs of defiance, stamping their feet at Nap as he inches ever nearer to them. They're letting him know it's not going to be easy. Firstly, all four sheep make a determined attempt to get away before being rounded up and calmly brought back to the pen. Then one bold sheep makes a bid for freedom. Again, Nap quietly ushers her back to the others, and before long the sheep are securely shut in the pen. 'They're stubborn, these Mule sheep,' Dave explains. 'They'll face a dog up. They won't back down. He has to show who's in charge. And he did.'

Finally, showing patience, Nap completes his run by skilfully shedding two sheep. The judge shouts 'That'll do,' and handler and dog are done. 'We had a good finish,' Dave says. 'If it wasn't for the mistake at the drive gates, it would have been a very good run. As it was I'd call it a fair run, but not as good as I'd have liked. They're very unpredictable things, these sheepdog trials. A lot of different factors come into play. The sheep have a lot to do with it. Sometimes they just toddle along and make your life easy. Sometimes they can fly all over the field and give you a lot of problems. The sheep were fine today, but you have to be alert, because you never quite know what they're going to do next.'

Watching Dave at work, few people realise that the whistle he uses from time to time isn't the mass-produced plastic kind used by other shepherds but a home-made version which is almost unique. Cut out of a tin (baby milk is the best) it's a small oblong piece of tin folded over into a V with a hole hammered into it. Filed down to remove any rough edges, the whistle fits neatly onto the tip of the little finger on Dave's left hand and when he lifts it to his lips it emits a piercing noise.

'The old shepherds just used to use quiet voice commands, and not very many of them,' Dave says. 'Even when it was windy and the dog was a long way away they still used voice commands. If they whistled it was just to stop the dog at the top of the field.

'I could whistle tremendously well with my fingers, but when I was in my early 20s I had all my teeth taken out by a dentist and found I couldn't whistle at all. It was a bit of a disaster, because I was deeply involved in dog trials, so I had to take drastic action. In desperation I went into the workshop and concocted a bit of tin with a hole in it, and I discovered I could whistle as loudly with that as I could with my fingers. It's just the same principle – you have to have your tongue in the right place and it carries just as well as a whistle performed with the fingers.

You can turn it up or turn it down, and get a shrill sound when you want it.'

People use sheepdog whistles made from all sorts of different materials, including bone and buffalo horn, but Dave's happy with his own invention. 'It's not a secret,' he says, 'but I've never seen anyone else use a whistle like mine. I just walk onto the trial field, whip it out of my pocket and use it. I suppose you could call it an original. It's not something I've ever discussed with anybody. It's just something that works for me.'

Having done his stint as releaser of sheep, and with one of his dogs' runs under his belt, Dave feels it might be time to listen to something other than whistles and shouts. While the trial continues he heads off to the nearby market town of Rothbury to do what shepherds have always traditionally done – listen to some music. He's arranged to meet shepherding colleague Robert Mackay at one of the pubs where music-making is taking place.

Bar staff with trays of drinks weave in and out of the customers basking on the lawn at the back of The Turk's Head. An impressive range of musical instruments is being unearthed from worn containers and fingered lovingly as a jam session gets under way. Banjos, fiddles, guitars and accordions lead the way. Flutes and penny whistles join in. A smartly-dressed young man from Newcastle chips in with the spoons. Happy in the warmth, visitors tap their feet and hum the tunes. Dave, who likes the occasional 'nip', is conscious of the drink-drive laws – and the need to stay focused for his second run at the sheepdog trials later in the day. So he sips a shandy and soaks up the atmosphere.

A murmur goes through the crowd as a tall man carrying a box eases his way through the throng to join the knot of musicians jamming steadily away. People recognise Alistair Anderson, concertina player of international repute and a driving force behind this mid-summer musical gathering. Alistair unpacks his black-and-silver instrument and launches into a jaunty version of a traditional Northumberland tune. The volume increases as more people join in. Soon you feel as though you are surrounded by an orchestra of traditional instruments. There's a feeling of contentment as the sun beats down and music swirls around the garden.

Rothbury Traditional Music Festival – Alistair is its chairman – is an annual gathering of musicians, singers and dancers. Now in its 20th year, the festival lasts for three days over the second weekend in July, attracting music-making people from all over the country. A ceilidh in the Jubilee Hall on the Friday night gets everyone in the mood for the Saturday, when there's a whole range of different events. Various venues stage competitions for fiddle, accordion, Northumberland pipes, lowland pipes, Highland pipes, drumming, dialect poetry, traditional singing, whistle, recorder and flute. Expert musicians hold workshops for aspiring pipes players, flute players, fiddle players and singers.

Next to the Market Cross crowds gather to watch groups of dancers. The main attraction this time is a group of men from Lancashire who rejoice in the name of the Britannia Bacup Coconutters. These colourfully-clad entertainers from the small Pennine town of Bacup, situated between Rochdale and Burnley, whirl their way through seven different dances. Five are performed in square sets with the dancers holding aloft arched garlands decorated in red, blue and white flowers. These are time-honoured dances connected with the renewed planting of crops in the spring. The group also performs a dance in which each member sports wooden discs on his hands, knees and belt. Like the pads miners wear when working in narrow seams, these discs or 'nuts' are struck in time with the music. To complete an extraordinary display, the men's faces are blackened. Some say this reflects their mining background, while others contend it stems from the need for a disguise to stop dancers being recognised by evil spirits. Whatever the origin, it gives the men a fearsome look. For hill shepherds like Dave and Robert, a group of men in fancy clothes gyrating their way through a series of ritual dances might be a bit difficult to take. But they accept it's all part of the festival mixture, a mixture which gets headier as the day wears on.

There's been a connection between shepherding and music for as long as there have been sheep in the valleys and hills. Marooned in their cottages far from their nearest neighbours, shepherds and their families were forced to make their own entertainment and many became accomplished musicians, handing down tunes learned from their fathers and grandfathers in days gone by. Very little of this music was written down, with the result that when shepherds died their musical memories went with them. In the 1980s Alistair Anderson, realising a musical tradition was at risk of disappearing, encouraged three old musicians to get together and perform as 'The Shepherds': Joe Hutton played Northumberland pipes, Willy Taylor fiddle, and Will Atkinson mouth organ. All three had spent a lifetime working on farms in the area, often walking long distances at night to play their music, helping to keep the traditional music of Northumberland and the Borders alive by playing at dances in village halls and concerts in rural schools.

Alistair arranged for The Shepherds to go on tour so that their music could be appreciated by a wider audience, he also encouraged them to make recordings of their music and books were published of the tunes they played. Will Atkinson's tune book came out shortly before he died, aged 95, in 2003. (Joe and Willy had pre-deceased him by a number of years.)

Unaccompanied singing is another skill kept alive by shepherds, one of whom makes an appearance at The Turk's Head to give a rendition of his favourite song. Graham Dick, born and bred at Great Tosson at the foot of the Simonside Hills, tends thirteen hundred sheep at Thockrington Farm near Hexham. He's been singing since he was five and is a regular entertainer at shepherds' suppers, Burns nights, concerts and farmers' gatherings. He's keen on dialect poetry too. The poem 'Canny Shepherd Laddie' is a salute to the Cheviot shepherds and their resilience. It starts like this:

> *Now there's songs about our soldiers and our sailors by the score*
> *And the tinkers and the tailors and other men galore*
> *But I'll sing you a wee bit ditty that you've never heard before*
> *About the canny shepherd laddie of the hills.*

It's one of Dave Baxter's favourite songs and along with the rest of the crowd gathered in the beer garden he joins in for the chorus:

> *Oh the shepherds of the Coquet and the Alwin and the Rede*
> *The Bowmont and the Breamish, they are all the same breed*
> *With his collie dog beside him and his stick with horned heed*
> *That's the canny shepherd laddie of the hills.*

Dave, who's worked in four of the five Cheviot valleys listed in the song, would like to hear more from Graham Dick. But it's time to get back to the dog trial at Flotterton.

As it happens, Dave misses his allotted turn and it's late afternoon before he gets to run his second dog, Scott. The ability of shepherds to see long distances is legendary, but his good eyesight doesn't help Dave on this occasion. The sun is low in the sky and he has to cup his hand over his eyes to cut out the glare. There's always the hope that, if your first dog doesn't perform as well as it should, your second will. But mistakes at the drive gates and the pen mean that when the time comes to hand out the prize money and present the cups neither Nap nor Scott are among the leaders this time. 'It's been a beautiful day and I've enjoyed meeting my friends and running my dogs,' Dave says. 'It's nice to do well and get placed, but that doesn't always happen. You just take it as it comes.'

Observers sometimes ask how it affects sheep who are being persuaded by shepherd and dog – not always as calmly as might be hoped – to follow the route round a trial field. Is there in any way a hint of the circus about the whole proceedings? The ISDS says not. The aim is to move the sheep as steadily as possible so as to cause no distress. Sheep chosen for the occasion must be healthy and fully able to undertake the walk round the trial field. When they have finished they are led to a quiet meadow to be reunited with the rest of the flock and continue their normal life. They only do the course once.

Dave reckons it isn't everyone who can make a good sheepdog handler. His view is simple. 'You've either got the knack, or you haven't,' he says. And bringing a dog to a trial requires a certain kind of trust. 'Your dogs have got to be friends with you when you come to these events. They mustn't be biters or make nuisances of themselves, because it can cause a great deal of trouble. You've got to have them under good control.'

Scott Smith, the Border Collie breeder from whom Dave bought his pup Meg, is also competing at the Flotterton sheepdog trial. He says that trials in Northumberland still manage to attract a reasonable field of competitors. But those in other areas, such as the Borders, are not doing so well as shepherds become thinner on the ground. Scott is aware of changes in the countryside and their effect on the people who look after Britain's flocks. 'Experienced people like Dave Baxter, who has a terrific record not just as a shepherd but also in handling Border Collies in a very natural way, are not going to continue that sort of way in the future. Because a lot of the bigger flocks now, especially on the hills, are herded by quad bikes with the dog jumping on the front or the back. So a lot of the natural instincts of the dog are, to some extent, being lost. And that's sometimes obvious with the way some of those dogs run on the trial field. Some of their outruns aren't quite the same. And I think, yes, the number of shepherds in the hills will decline. They're going to look after fewer sheep, and that in itself will have a knock-on effect. We'll end up having fewer people in the hills.'

It's not a new development. But it's one which Scott regrets. 'I think the depopulation of the countryside is going to continue, as will the deterioration of the more remote areas of Northumberland. There will be fewer children, fewer schools, fewer buses and poorer services. It's very sad to see this trend. But it's probably inevitable.'

∾

Shear Skill

A sultry afternoon at the beginning of July. The occasional shaft of sunlight pierces the clouds and lights up a patch of ground on the shoulder of a distant hill. Hill shepherds call these splashes of brightness on the landscape 'haymakers' because they often herald good haymaking weather.

Dave has no plans to make hay at the moment. He's busy building a small fire in a brazier that he's made from an old oil can. But the fact that the weather looks settled for the next few days is important because it's clipping day at Linshiels, one of several as Dave and Robert MacKay, the shepherd at another farm run by Dave's employers, shear their way through the 800 ewes and 200 ewe hoggs that roam the farm's 3,000 acres. And keeping the sheep dry is essential for this annual task.

There's a right time to clip the sheep. As the old saying warns, don't start on your lowland sheep too early in the year:

> *Shear your sheep in May*
> *And shear them all away.*

The same advice is given for hill sheep:

> *Clip hill ewes in June*
> *Clip them far too soon.*

But, having said that, don't leave it too late, either. Here in Coquetdale the right time for shearing sheep tends to be July. As for the fire that Dave's stoking up? That's to heat the branding irons used to mark the horns on some of the sheep after they've been shorn.

Sheep have been parted from their fleeces for as long as they've been tended by man.

The first farmers quickly realised that shearing had to be done every summer – for purely practical reasons. If the old wool isn't removed from a sheep's body most of it eventually drops off anyway as the new fleece starts to grow underneath. So it might as well be properly harvested.

One of the earliest references to removing the wool from sheep comes in the Old Testament (Genesis 31, 19) where Jacob comes across flocks of sheep owned by his uncle Laban in what is today part of northern Syria: 'And Laban went eagerly to shear his sheep,' the Bible recounts. It seems that, even then, shearing festivals were an occasion for celebrating.

Sheep-shearing is mentioned in Roman literature in a pronouncement by Emperor Tiberius (42 BC to 37 AD). His reply to certain provincial Roman governors, who were keen to impose ever-heavier taxes on their subjects, was: 'It is the duty of a good shepherd to shear his sheep, not to flay them'. It's evident that sheep-shearing was a well-established practice in Roman times and, although we're not entirely sure what kind of fleece-cutting tools the Roman shepherds used, it's thought to have been some rudimentary form of shears. These continued to be used for centuries after the Romans left Britain, but it wasn't until the late 18th century that the spring-tined hand shears we recognise today became available on an industrial scale. These have two triangular scissor-shaped blades jutting from handles connected by a loop of spring steel. When the shearer's hand squeeze the blades, they cut the wool before springing apart again, ready for the next snip. Over the last 200 years millions of sheep all over the world have been shorn with hand-shears based on this simple design. And some still continue to be clipped that way today.

As mentioned earlier, the wealth of England in the Middle Ages owed much to the country's dominance as a trader in the

European wool market, and as a result wool came to have a symbolic role in the pomp and ceremony of one of our most important institutions. The large bag of wool covered with red cloth stowed beneath the Lord Chancellor's seat in the House of Lords is known as the Woolsack. Introduced by Edward III (1327–77), it was originally stuffed with English wool as a reminder of England's traditional source of wealth and as a sign of prosperity. Today, it's filled with wool from each of the countries of the Commonwealth, to symbolise unity.

The degree to which England exploited its position as Europe's premier wool producer can be gleaned from Exchequer records which show that in 1354, the 28th year of Edward III's reign, this country exported 31,651 sacks of wool and 3,036 hundredweights (150 tonnes) of 'fells' (sheepskins). Sixty ships sailed from Southampton alone, laden with wool for the Netherlands.

Sadly, the pre-eminence that wool enjoyed in our economy in the past is not matched by its position today. Our wool still has a value, but it's disappointingly low. In 2002–03 the average price realised by the UK clip was 73.4p per kilo, whereas South African sheep farmers got 302.8p, Australian 282.6p and New Zealand 156.6p. There are a number of reasons for the discrepancy, one being that quite a large proportion of the UK's wool comes from breeds of sheep – including some from our hill areas – whose fleeces are not considered to be of good enough quality for today's market. This drags down the overall average price.

Whatever the economics of wool production today, sheep still have to be shorn, just as they have been for centuries. There have, however, been some big changes in the way it's done. Even as recently as 50 years ago shearing days were a highlight of the midsummer months on farms throughout Britain. They were companionable occasions which brought a great deal of pleasure to the farm staff who worked with sheep all the year round but rarely wandered far from home. At shearing time farmers and their workers would move from one farm to another in their district, helping to shear their neighbour's sheep. No money changed hands, it was all done on goodwill. A timetable was drawn up listing which flocks in the locality were to be clipped and when it would take place, so that the sheep could be gathered and ready. If it rained and sheep on one farm got wet, they moved to the back of the queue to wait until the animals on all the remaining farms had been clipped. With so many sheep to gather in turn, the plan had to be adhered to.

Meanwhile, farmers' wives would vie with one another to see who could lay on the biggest banquet. They took pride in the mountains of bread, pies and cakes they baked to feed the men and boys who thronged the pens, catching sheep and clipping their wool, marking their newly-shaven flanks and wrapping their fleeces. When the day was over, jugs of cider and beer, often brewed specially for the occasion, would appear. Musical instruments would be removed from their cases and everyone would join in the dancing and the singing. In some ways, shepherds were the last among rural workers to preserve these convivial traditions. As far back as 1827 the writer William Home noted that practices like 'harvest home', where the last sheaf was ceremoniously paraded from the field and a dance was held to celebrate the end of a successful harvest, were 'sinking into disuse as a scene of mirth and revelry' and that only sheep-shearings remained as occasions where festivities took place.

The journalist and novelist Elizabeth Gaskell (1810–65) wrote about many aspects of rural life in Victorian England. In 1853 she published an account of a visit to a hill farm a few miles from Keswick in the Lake District. Perched on the side of a hill on the east side of Derwentwater the farm had spectacular views over Maiden Moor, Cat Bells and Causey Pike. A crowd of local farming folk had gathered to help with the clipping of a large number of Herdwicks. These distinctive Lakeland sheep, with their white faces and coarse grey fleeces, have a long history: according to some, they were brought into Britain by Norse settlers in the tenth century. But others claim they were introduced by Cistercian monks at Furness Abbey near Barrow-in-Furness at a later time. A slow-maturing breed of sheep, their meat was considered to be so tasty that it was known as 'the king's mutton'.

Gathered in a large mob, the Herdwicks presented an impressive sight to the visiting author. So too did the men who were about to clip them:

'The flock of sheep to be shorn on this occasion consisted of more than a thousand, and eleven famous shearers had come, walking in from many miles' distance to try their skill one against the other; for sheep-shearings are a sort of rural Olympics. They were all young men in their prime, strong, and well-made; without coat or waistcoat, and with upturned shirt-sleeves. They sat each across a long bench or narrow table, and caught up the sheep from the attendant boys, who had dragged it in; they lifted it on to the bench, and placing it by a dexterous knack on its back, they began to shear the wool off the tail and under parts; then they tied the two hind legs and the two fore legs together, and laid it first on one side and then on the other, till the fleece came off in one whole piece; the art was to shear all the wool off, and yet not to injure the sheep by any awkward cut: if such an accident did occur, a mixture of tar and butter was immediately applied; but every wound was a blemish on the shearer's fame.'

The competitive nature of shearers was clearly as fierce in Elizabeth Gaskell's time as it is today:

'To shear well and completely, and yet to do it quickly, shows the perfection of the clippers. Some can finish off as many as six score sheep in a summer's day; and if you consider the weight and uncouthness of the animal, and the general heat of the weather, you will see that, with justice, clipping or shearing is regarded as harder work than mowing. But most good shearers are content with despatching four or five score; it is only on unusual occasions that six score are attempted or accomplished.'

There is an equally graphic description of a clipping day in Thomas Hardy's *Far From the Madding Crowd* which was published in 1874. The shearing on this occasion is carried out by six burly men in a 400-year-old barn that boasts a thrashing floor of 'thick oak, black with age and polished by the beating of flails for many generations till it had grown as slippery and as rich in hue as the stateroom floor of an Elizabethan mansion.'

Whereas the shearers in Elizabeth Gaskell's Lakeland description are using stools, or forms, to clip their sheep on, (other dialect words were 'stocks', 'creels' or 'cratches') those in Hardy's novel kneel as they work, with 'the sun slanting in upon their bleached shirts, tanned arms and polished shears, causing these to bristle with a thousand rays, enough to blind a weak-eyed man.'

It's worth noting in passing the prices farmers were getting for their Herdwick wool in Cumberland (now part of Cumbria) in the middle of 19th century. One man complained to Elizabeth Gaskell in 1853 that there had been a slump in returns in recent years. He expected to get about twelve shillings (60p) a stone (six kilos), which works out at about 10p a kilo in today's values. A few years earlier 'before that Australian wool started coming in' he was receiving twice as much (£1 a stone). It underlines the impact on world wool prices that the explosion in sheep farming in Australia had in the 19th century. In 1800 the country had a mere 6,000 head of sheep but 80 years later the number had soared to 60 million. Moreover, the wool produced by Australian Merino sheep was vastly superior.

Until the first couple of decades of the 20th century many sheep farmers in Britain persisted in washing their flocks before having them clipped. Part of the idea was to encourage the rise of the new wool which lifted the fleece from the skin of the sheep and made it easier to clip. It was generally agreed that, for this exercise, flowing water was better than a pond:

> *Wash sheep for the better where water doth run*
> *And let them go cleanly and dry in the sun'*
> Thomas Tusser 1593

The year 1771 saw the publication of the *Farmer's Kalender* 'containing plain instructions for performing the work of various kinds of farms in every season of the year'. In this journal, advice about washing was unequivocal: 'The sheep must be washed in a pool or river, taking the opportunity of a warm day. The only rule in doing this work is to wash them until the wool is quite clean and white. Some people have a notion it will kill the fish in a pond, but this is mere vulgar error: on the contrary, the vermin that are washed out will feed the fish well.'

As a convenient spot to wash their sheep farmers often used a stream or river running through their land. Washing was usually done about nine to ten days before clipping. On the whole, a better price was paid for the washed wool, so although with the soil rinsed out it weighed less (and they were paid by weight as well as quality) it was considered a worthwhile practice. Places called Sheepwash, Washbrook or Washfold can be seen on old maps and these names stem from a river, stream or ford where sheep-washing traditionally took place.

Before washing began, lambs were shed from their mothers and held in a nearby field while the ewes were driven down to the water's edge where a temporary pen was constructed from hurdles. The stream was dammed with something like an old barn door held in place with stones and turf sods. Soon a large pool was formed and bathing could begin. The sheep were dragged from the pen and heaved towards the washing-man who stood where the water was deepest. Carrying out this unenviable task was often the fate of the farm lad or apprentice shepherd, and soaking him with the splashes made by the sheep as they landed in the 'bath' was a popular game and a source of endless amusement to the onlookers. After the soil and dirt had been washed from a fleece by the first washer, the sheep was passed to a second man who turned it on its back and immersed it once again. All the while, the shepherd, who generally felt himself to be above the menial task of dunking sheep, would stand in the shallows casting a critical eye over the waterlogged animals as they struggled out of the pool and headed for the safety of the fields on the opposite side of the stream.

On some farms, the washers kept reasonably dry by standing in a barrel fixed to posts which had been driven into the bed of the stream, but in most places they just stood in the water. To keep warm, they would wear two pairs of old trousers and a sack tied round about their waist. But two hours in a stream fed by freezing water straight off the fells was usually as much as they could bear and stand-by washers would have to take their place while they thawed out on the river bank. There was some debate at the time over the long-term effects that washing days had on those who stood in an icy stream for lengthy periods. Farmers who became crippled and bent in their later years were inclined to blame their afflictions on days spent washing sheep in their youth.

Like clipping days, washings were festive occasions to which friends, relatives and children were invited. People came from far away to help sort out the sheep and have them ready for washing. Women lugged baskets containing copious amounts of food and drink to the place where the sheep were gathered and white table-cloths would be spread out on the grass for the gang of washers to sit around, feasting on the home-made fare. In the evening, there would be games and sports, and on farms where drinking wasn't frowned upon the whisky bottle would be passed round and tales of farming in days gone by would be told and re-told.

The washing days are no more and more than 130 years have elapsed since Hardy wrote his account of a Wessex clipping day. Yet in some ways the scene at Linshiels on this sultry summer afternoon retains some of the features of those far-off times: a wooden floor, polished by the scrabblings of thousands of sheep's feet; a series of corridors, alleyways and races funnelling sheep into a catching pen; lambs bleating to be reunited with their mothers; dogs barking in sporadic bursts; shearers bending over their sheep as the wool falls in drifts onto the floor; fleeces being carefully rolled.

The biggest change is in the speed the whole operation takes. The careful clipping of a ewe with hand shears will take on average five minutes, depending on the sheep and the rise of the fleece. With machine shears, shaped like a barber's clippers, it'll take about a fifth of that. It means that fewer shearers are needed to clip the same number of sheep. This may be progress, but it amounts to another nail in the shepherd's coffin.

Of course, clipping has been transformed since mechanical shears were developed at the end of the 19th century. In the early years they were hand-driven, the shearer (or his assistant) turning a handle which set in motion a series of cogs and connecting rods leading to a cable. At the end of the cable was a clipping comb similar to those used today, its reciprocating teeth chewing their way through the fleece. When the operator stopped turning the handle the head stopped cutting. The machine looked rather top-heavy with its single tubular leg supported by a metal tripod, but it had the advantage of being portable and could be used in pens away from the farm, whereas the electric machines which soon followed relied on the clippers having a source of power.

One of the pioneers of the new range of clipping machines was the Wolseley Sheep Shearing Company, which was founded in 1887 in Sydney, Australia, by Frederick York Wolseley. In 1893 he moved the firm to Birmingham but by 1906 he and his staff had lost interest in producing shearing machines and had started on a much more glamorous enterprise: designing and building cars. Another leader in the shearing machine world was the Stewart Company, and there are illustrated adverts for their range of shearing equipment in the farming press and sheep farming publications in the early years of the 20th century. Four pounds, nineteen shillings and sixpence (just under £5) would buy a hand-driven device and, for those prepared to pay a bit more, an electric machine could be had for six pounds, one shilling and sixpence (£6.07p).

A fleece, once separated from its source, should be in one piece. And that's generally the case, except when the animal has been suffering from some ailment or other. A mineral deficiency, for example, will cause the wool to hang in strips from the animal's body before falling off altogether. For a fleece not to be penalised by the buyer it must be properly wrapped, the sides turned in and the fleece wrapped as tight as a bunkroll. Until 1988, a wool rope was twisted from the neck of the fleece and secured round the rolled-up bundle, but this 'neckband' is no longer insisted upon, which helps to speed up the wrapping process.

Rolling the fleeces at Linshiels is Lesley Anderson, daughter of the tenant of the farm, Mary Carruthers. Lesley's at full stretch as Dave and Robert shear away, giving their startled sheep the appearance of Army conscripts sporting a Number One haircut. A raddle (colour-mark) on each sheep's flank is applied, using a stick, before it's released. As she completes the wrapping of each fleece Lesley drops it in a large polyethylene sack suspended from a metal frame. These wool 'sheets', as they're called, used to be made of hessian and hold between 65 and 75 kilos of wool – the equivalent of between 25 and 30 Blackface fleeces. Pillowcase-shaped, they must have been easy to fit over the back of a pony or a horse, the only transport in the days before lorries linked the countryside to the towns and delivered the fleeces to the woollen mills.

The metal frame was constructed by a local blacksmith: it makes the wool sheet much easier to handle than suspending it from a couple of beams, which is often the solution in murky farm buildings. Periodically, Lesley presses down the fleeces to get more in, until finally the sheet is full and Dave, using a technique learned as a shepherd boy 50 years ago, sews up the mouth of the bag with a fierce-looking packing needle and a length of twine. It's a fair guess that it's the only sewing he's done in his life, but it has to be done right: purchasers like their wool sheets sewn up with one continuous piece of string knotted at either end. 'Safe bind, safe find' is the motto.

In due course this day's clip, together with the rest of the fleeces from the farm's flock, will be collected by the buyer's lorry and transported to a warehouse to be divided into different grades. This buyer is the British Wool Marketing Board, which was set up as a farmers' organisation in 1950. In its first 40 years wool producers received a government subsidy in the form of a guaranteed price and this arrangement effectively ironed out the peaks and troughs in a wool market which can be extremely volatile. Then, 13 years ago, the guaranteed system was abolished and today the board is run as a farmers' co-operative receiving no payment from the State. It is non-profit-making, returning all the proceeds of sales – less costs – to the producers.

In terms of output the UK is a small player in a dauntingly large world market. Australia, according to the latest figures, produces 439 million kilos of wool a year; New Zealand 185 million kilos; China 145 million kilos; and the UK (in fourth place) 42 million kilos. The UK clip is very mixed since we have more breeds and cross-breeds than any other country, moreover the amounts of wool from individual farms are relatively small so having a centralised marketing system such as that run by the BWMB is crucial to wool producers and buyers alike.

The pattern of wool production over the last 40-odd years is a useful guide as to why the number of shepherds – on both lowland and hill farms – has plummeted. In the early 1960s there were about 130,000 farmers with flocks containing something like 30 million sheep. The total wool output from these farms was 35 million kilos. In 2002–03 there were half the number of farmers (61,000) and their flocks totalled 35 million sheep and the wool output has remained at 35 million kilos. So, although the number of flocks has fallen by half, the number of sheep and the output of wool have stayed the same. There are no precise figures on the reduction of paid labour on sheep farms and many of the flocks which have vanished will have been small units employing no staff, but the disappearance of 65,000 flocks must surely have resulted in the loss of several thousand shepherds' jobs.

In a valley like the Upper Coquet, where all the holdings are sheep farms, the Wool Board will try to collect all the wool being clipped by the likes of Dave and Robert on the same day. The Board, however, is duty bound to collect wool from all flocks with more than four sheep. So to keep costs down in areas where there are fewer flocks and the amounts of wool are smaller, producers are urged to drop off their packed wool sheets at a collection centre.

So what happens to those Blackface fleeces that are being so carefully packed by Lesley at Linshiels? That wool sheet, along with the 150,000 other sheets which are sent out by the Wool Board, ends up at one of a network of BWMB depots where the raw product is graded fleece by fleece before being packed into large bales holding the same type and quality. The 'graders' who perform this skilful task develop an astonishingly sensitive touch for wool and can tell the age of a sheep from its fleece. It used to be said that a really experienced grader could pluck a wisp of wool from a barbed wire fence and know from feeling it what condition the sheep was in.

Before the Wool Board was formed, many farmers would take a sample of their wool to 'wool fairs' in nearby market towns. There they would negotiate a price with a merchant, who then sent sheets to collect the remainder of the clip. Most merchants came from long-established families whose connections with the wool trade went back centuries. They were key members of the agricultural supply industry, selling a whole range of requisites to the farmers they bought the wool from. They had to be wily, too. Some farmers would try to conceal inferior wool by surrounding it with higher-grade fleeces, and merchants had to be alert to the possibility of malpractice.

Every year the BWMB organises regular auctions in Bradford where the wool is sold to the textile trade. A sample of the wool from each bale is taken prior to the sale and sent to a laboratory to be analysed for colour, fibre thickness and grease content. Potential buyers study the results of these tests before the auction-eer invites them to compete for the wool in bids of pence and half-pence per kilo. Once they have purchased the wool they need, buyers transport the bales to a processing plant to be washed or 'scoured'. Raw wool is coated in grease and may contain mud, seeds and thorns from the countryside where the sheep grazed, but that soon changes once scouring begins. After passing through a succession of baths containing detergent and hot water the wool is rinsed, squeezed through rollers and dried. Astonishingly, wool loses almost a third of its weight when the

Above: Blindburn Farm a hundred years ago. No cottages then – the shepherds all lodged in the big house.

Below: Uswayford in the Cheviot Hills a hundred years ago. The 'lonely farm' where Dave and Mona met.

Above: Yearning Hall, Upper Coquetdale in 1910. Now just a ruin, the farm was home to a family of eight in those days.

YEARNING HALL UPPER COQUET

MAIN STREET, ROTHBURY.

Above: A shepherd taking his flock through the streets of Rothbury in Northumberland on his way to an autumn sheep sale in 1908.

Above: Clipping Day at Barrowburn in the Upper Coquet valley in the early 1900s. A horse waits patiently as fleeces are piled onto the cart.

Below: Shearers, catchers and wrappers: the whole family joins in at the clipping. Rooklands Farm in the Cheviot Hills at the end of the 19th century.

Above: A mid-summer scene from the 1890s. A farmer and his shepherds preparing to wash sheep in a pool at the source of the River Derwent high on North York Moors. Farmers were paid a bonus for wool that had been washed.

Above: The busy scene at Rothbury Mart in 1905, where pens are packed with Cheviot sheep. Rothbury no longer operates as a live-stock mart and the pens stand empty. But the auction ring is still used for sales of fine art and furniture.

Below: A sheep may safely graze. While watching his flock with his dog by his side, a shepherd is visited by his daughter. A picture taken at Glaisdale near Whitby, North Yorkshire, in the 1890s.

PARISH OF WOLSINGHAM,
DURHAM.

275.—THOMAS DAWSON, *Fine.*—Horn burn, T D on each horn ; tar mark, Ewes and Young Sheep, D on the far side ; Two-year-old Sheep, D on the far side, and a stroke on the near side ; Three-year-old Sheep, D on the far side, and two strokes down the near side.

276.—THOMAS NEWTON, *Coves Houses.*—Horn burn, N on the near, and 2 on the far horn ; tar mark, Old Sheep, N on the far side ; Two-year-old Sheep, N on the near side ; and Young Sheep, N on each side.

277.—JOHN HANKEY, *Ape Shield.*—Horn burn, I H ; near ear stowed ; far ear forked ; tar mark, a stroke from the middle of the back to the cameral, on the near side, and H on the far side:—Bought Sheep.—Horn burn, I H ; tar mark, a stroke on the far side, the same as above, and H on the near side.

Right: A Shepherds' Meet in the Lake District in 1900. On specific dates throughout the year the men got together at convenient meeting spots (often a pub) where they restored stray sheep collected from the fells to their proper owners. To make sure the animals went back to the right farm, the organisers usually used a Shepherd's Guide.

Above: Making their mark. A typical page from an old Shepherd's Guide showing the horn burns, ear marks and tar marks of three flocks from the Wolsingham district in the North Pennines.

Right: Shepherds with their dogs posing on shearing stools as they await the start of a clipping day. A photograph taken at Bowes in Co. Durham at the end of the 19th century.

Above: A shepherd from the Borders of Scotland in characteristic garb. Shod in tacketty boots, he is wrapped in his traditional plaid, the length of tweed 'herds wore to keep themselves warm in all weathers. The man is standing in front of a makeshift lambing hut roofed in turf sods and pine branches. The picture dates from the 1880s.

grease is removed, but there are uses for the grease: it's purified to make lanolin used in face cream, hand cream, soap and ointment.

By now, the wool is clean and white but extremely tangled. The next stage in its treatment is to feed it into a carding machine where rollers covered with tiny wire teeth untangle the fibres and remove any pieces of hay or straw which may still contaminate the product. Wool to be used for worsted yarn is combed on a machine which runs the fibres through a series of teeth, removing all the short fibres and teasing out the longer ones to lie smooth and parallel with one another. The wool is then combed into a rope which is wound into a 'ball' or 'bump' ready for spinning. Wool destined for woollen yarn is not combed but left higgledy piggledy ready for spinning. The sliver of wool – combed or tangled – is passed on to a series of machines which twist and draw out the fibres into a continuous thread of the right thickness. Worsted yarn is spun more tightly and is stronger than woollen yarn.

That wool has to be subjected to so many processes is one reason why the BWMB constantly urges farmers to present their fleeces in the best possible condition. Over the years the board has urged producers not to be too liberal with the 'bloom' dips used to make show sheep more attractive. There used to be a tiny market for 'daggs', the soiled wool clipped from around a sheep's behind, but that's vanished and the board no longer collects them. In fact, it imposes a 10p per kilo 'fine' if wool sheets contain daggs. And there are other penalties, too. For instance, 10p per kilo is deducted for unwrapped fleeces and 30p per kilo for sending in wool which contains polypropylene twine, because if that slipped through the system it would have devastating results.

These measures are accepted by producers as necessary

attempts to improve the quality of fleeces offered for sale. But the price farmers receive for their wool is so low that, quite under-standably, they tend to give it scant attention. At one time, farmers reckoned the wool cheque covered the rent, but not any longer. The return on the wool from some hill breeds is less than £1.50 a head, and the costs of shearing often exceed that. Producers say it's a case of clipping their sheep because they have to, not because there's much financial incentive. Things have come a long way since the Second World War when every wisp of wool was wanted. In those days, even 'fallen wool', the fleece on a dead sheep, was saved. It was either clipped from the body after rigor mortis had set in or plucked from the corpse when it started to 'ripen'. Scavengers, who toured the farms looking for some-thing to buy, would pay sixpence a sack (two and a half pence) for fallen wool. They also bought dirty wool collected from around the farm, which they washed and sold to local wool merchants. In those days, every bit counted.

Another long-standing custom has vanished from the wool trade in the last century. This is the tradition whereby sheep farmers by-passed the middle man and took their wool straight to a local mill. By way of payment the farmer received woollen items for his family, while the mill owner benefited from a regular supply of locally-grown wool. One mill where this was done was that owned by the Waddell family on the banks of the River Rede at Otterburn in Northumberland where, in 1821, William Waddell of Jedburgh, the younger member of a respectable family of wool manufacturers brought his young bride, 17-year-old Charlotte Ferrier, with whom he had eloped (scandalously, Charlotte had absconded from the fashionable 'School For Young Ladies' in George Square in Edinburgh).

The textile trade was one of the first to benefit from the Industrial Revolution and at the start of the 19th century a string of woollen mills were built by landlords in towns and villages close to sheep-rearing areas where they could profit from locally produced wools. William, undaunted by the prospect of a crippling 109-year-lease whose terms precluded any substantial expansion, took on one of these mills and, aided by his wife, their ever-increasing family, and a small local workforce, took in the wool fleeces from local farmers and in return supplied them with blankets, cloth or knitting yarn – whatever woollen goods they required. The wool bought by the Waddells was converted to yarn in the mill and sent to the local hand-loom weavers, who produced the blankets and cloth. The woven products were returned to the mill to be washed and finished.

There are people in the area who still have dim memories of their ancestors proudly wearing garments woven from their own wool at Otterburn Mill. But those days are long gone. Today, two-thirds of the UK wool clip is used in carpets but the UK carpet industry has had its difficulties in recent years and the Wool Board has been trying to develop new markets abroad. The Belgian carpet industry is the largest overseas market for British wool and there are signs that manufacturers there are beginning to reduce their reliance on synthetic products and are turning back to wool for making carpets and rugs. Interest is growing in British wool in China and Japan, too. And in the United States, where wool carpet currently represents just two per cent of the carpet industry, there are signs that British exporters are making inroads.

At the same time, the BWMB is striving to boost prices for the less popular wools. An example is grey Swaledale, which in 2002 accounted for more than 1.5 million kilos of British fleece wool. Since the move towards lighter colours in home furnishings, the demand for dark Swaledale wool for carpets has been poor – even though it's been praised in the past as good carpet wool. Now, using new technology, a technique has been developed which can lighten dark fibres, and this may boost demand for grey Swaledale wool. In another venture, the board is supporting a UK spinner in its campaign to persuade textile manufacturers on the West Coast of the United States to use coloured yarns, including Herdwick and grey Swaledale, in rug and broadloom carpet ranges which, it's hoped, will appeal to customers looking for a more natural product.

Looking ahead, the Wool Board is planning further research into new uses for wool which don't necessarily involve it being woven in the traditional way.

In the shearing shed at Linshiels Dave's harking back to his youth – and his early experience of clipping. He's picked out a gimmer to shear and he's going to use his much-cherished 'blades', the razor-sharp hand shears he's kept for many years. 'We were trained to use hand shears as young lads,' he recalls, 'and I like to get them out from time to time to keep the tradition going, because there's not many does it now. You're trying to get the fleece off without any damage to the sheep, simple as that. They've got to be sharp, your shears, so you have to keep them properly maintained.

'Hand shearing's just a thing you pick up as you go along. An old chap from Morebattle in Scotland taught me. He was one of those old boys who lived in the neighbourhood at the time, they called them "tramp clippers". They weren't tramps in the sense of them being vagrants; they got the name because they tramped round the countryside clipping. Anyway, he taught me to clip with the blades. He used to have rubbers on his to stop them making that clack-clack noise you make when you're snipping away at a fleece. He reckoned the clack disturbed the sheep.'

Nevertheless, there's a practical reason for Dave to practise his skills with hand shears. From time to time a ewe avoids being gathered up with the rest of the sheep on its hirsel, however good Dave's dogs might be. If she misses the gathering for the clipping, she's still got to be shorn. So, for a period in August the shepherd will take his shears with him on his rounds, and if he spots a sheep which still has its fleece he'll get the dogs to bring it to him and he'll shear it there and then on the hill. Similarly, on vast farms in remote areas like the west coast of Scotland, bunches of sheep which have been missed on gatherings will still be herded into a convenient corner and clipped by hand rather than go through the inconvenience of bringing them all the way down to the farm where there is a source of power.

There's one other group of people who still prefer to use hand shears. They're the 'hobby farmers' who only keep a handful of sheep, and they're happy to shell out £15 for a pair of shears and snip their way through their flock at a rate of one or two a day. It may take a fortnight for them to work through all their sheep, but many feel that being old-fashioned is somehow more 'natural'.

That's not to say the old method was slow, far from it. Clippers wielding hand shears could snip their way through a flock of sheep at a tidy pace. And they made sure that everything was geared towards ensuring a constant throughput. In some areas of the country a century ago, clippers used to bring an assistant to sharpen one set of shears while they continued to use their other pair. They brought their own whetstones encased in a small wooden box with a lid, and they'd either spit on the stone or tip a drop of oil onto it from a tiny oilcan before stropping away to restore the sharpness of the shears. Getting the 'edge' right on a set of shears is a skill in itself and not everyone could do it.

It was also known for clippers to give assistants a penny to go into the catching pen and bring them the sheep whose fleece had a good rise, so that they could keep up their clipping speed. A rate of three minutes each, or 20 an hour, or 160 a day was considered feasible with hill breeds like Blackfaces. In fact, the current British record for shearing by hand is 206 in nine hours. But for sheep with denser fleeces like Scotch Half-breeds, a figure of 80 a day was good going.

'Some of the old boys who were really good with the shears could clip a ewe pretty quickly,' Dave recalls. 'They were good shearers, those old boys. The machine clippers are fast, no one can dispute that. But hand shearing wasn't slow and the blades leave more wool on. That means the sheep have more protection on a bad night.'

Like most shepherds of his generation Dave, with 50 shearings under his belt, laments the passing of the old customs. 'Clipping days today are a lot harder, because there aren't as many shearers and there aren't as many people coming to help out, either. I remember when we had clipping days at this farm, Linshiels, about 15 men used to come to shear. Now there's just two and a wrapper for the fleeces. Maybe some of them weren't doing that much those days at the shearing, but it was tradition to come round and help your neighbours, see. That was just the way it went; on and on and on, for years. They were good crack, the clipping days. There used to be a big luncheon, then supper when you finished, and some of them got their breakfast too if they were there to help with the gathering.'

With fewer people working on farms there's been a growth in the number of shearing contractors in Britain. They may have worked as shepherds in the past, or they are the tenants of small farms with just a few score sheep who need to supplement their income. So in high summer they go on the road taking their shears with them. Some work single-handed, and often spend all year travelling round the world, shearing sheep in Australia, New Zealand, Norway and the Falkland Isles, as well as in the UK. Others stay in this country, working in gangs of two, three or four. The larger gangs are able to handle up to 100,000 sheep a year, the smaller ones 10,000.

A recent trend has been for contractors to take their own shearing trailers with them. The design of these varies. One popular version has a race with a decoy sheep at the front. Sheep, being curious, walk up the race towards the decoy in a line and are pulled, one by one, onto the clipping floor by the shearer. Such an arrangement does away with the need for someone to catch the sheep, so it frees the farmer to carry out other tasks with the sheep while they are gathered for the shearing.

There are 60 pure breeds in the UK, as well as many cross breeds, and sheep vary enormously in size. Some hulking specimens weigh as much as 80 to 90 kilos, while other daintier animals tip the scales at just 30 kilos. This range of animals has an effect on the rates charged by shearers. In some areas it's £1 a sheep, in others 75p. Shearers charge more if they're clipping pedigree sheep because they tend to be heavier and the flocks are smaller. And they charge less per sheep if it's a contract for a large flock.

In terms of speed of clipping, experience and physical ability clearly play their part, as well as the condition of the sheep. Dave puts it like this: 'Sheep that are fit are usually good to shear.' An average shearer will take about a minute to a minute and a half to clip a sheep, but in manhandling it into the shearing position and holding it to be marked afterwards a further 30 seconds may elapse, making it more like two minutes per sheep. That's 30 sheep an hour, or 240 for an eight-hour day. Of course, faster shearers can notch up a tally of 300 a day, and with hill flocks, like those at Linshiels and Blindburn containing Blackface, Swaledale or Cheviot sheep, some shearing contractors can manage 400 a day.

Some of the sheep being clipped at Linshiels are ewe hoggs, born 14 months ago and soon to become replacements for the older ewes in the flock. This is the first time they've been shorn and this is not the only first they will experience today: they will also be branded at the base of their horn with an identifying mark. Dave brings the iron over from the fire. 'Is't hot?' Robert asks. 'Aye,' chuckles Dave. 'Hot at both ends!' The heat has spread up the shaft of the iron and Dave has to wrap a piece of wool round the handle like a makeshift oven glove. A puff of smoke and the acrid smell of burnt horn confirms that the sheep has been branded. The figure 3 signifies 2003, the year it joined the flock as a hogg. Traditionally, shepherds also branded the other horn with a mark consisting of the initials of the owner or even his name, if it was short enough to fit. The chief reason was to identify a sheep if it strayed from its usual grazing area. It's a custom which has been going on for almost 300 years.

Some time in the early years of the 19th century two sheep farmers in the Keswick area of Cumberland were discussing how they could set up a register of flock keepers in the northern part of the Lake District when one suggested that they should send each other sketches of their own sheep with their various points of identification marked on the drawings. This was the conversation which led to the birth of a remarkable reference book, *The Shepherds Guide*, the first of which was compiled by Joseph Walker, a farmer from Martindale on Ullswater in 1817. It contained the 'proper delineation' of the burn marks, ear marks or wool marks of something like 2,000 flocks in four areas of the Northern Pennines and the Lake District. The aim was 'that everyone might have the power of knowing the owner of stray sheep and so be able to restore to every man his own'.

Ear or lug marks are patterns cut into the ears of sheep, usually when they are lambs. As the ear quickly heals, the mark becomes permanent. Each style has its own special term, for instance: 'under slitted', 'fold bitted', 'punch holed', 'ritted', or 'neck bitted'. These relate to the type of mark and the place on the ear where the mark is made.

The 'pop' or 'smit' marks are colour marks applied to various parts of the fleece, with a name describing a part of the body: for example, 'far hook' or 'near shoulder'. The marks, which these days are done with proprietary marking fluid, were originally made using haematite ore, graphite or tar. The combination of these ear and smit marks is unique to a particular farm and is part of its freehold.

Each page in *The Guide* lists a flock, its owner and farm of origin, with a sketch of a sheep and a description of the flock's various marks. Weighing about a pound and a half, the guide fits snugly into a large pocket, ready to be brought forth when needed.

The Guide also lays out a timetable for farmers to gather stray sheep on the moors or commons and take them to a 'shepherds' meet' at the foot of the fells. The dates of these get-togethers –

and the format of the occasion – are always the same. On a green next to a country inn pens are erected in which strays are held pending an examination of their marks. After the animals have been sorted out and given back to their rightful owners the organisers repair to the pub. This tradition, which also included a lavish tea, continued until foot and mouth disease ravaged the hefted flocks on many of the high hills in the North of England in 2001. Since then, many sheep farmers on those places have changed their livestock policy with the result that shepherds' meets, so enjoyed in the past, are in danger of fading away altogether through lack of interest.

Whether *The Guide* continues to be published also remains to be seen. Until now, this shepherds' Bible has come out roughly every ten years. The most recent issue of the 700-page tome was in 2000, and as usual entailed a huge amount of work for a small committee of people. An idiosyncratic publication, which mystifies all but the most knowledgeable, it is nevertheless part of the heritage of the northern Pennines and the Lake District hills and a plan needs to be put in place to sustain it to 2017, when it will be celebrating its centenary, and beyond.

The branding finished, Dave and Robert pause for a minute and lean against the polished wooden rails of the pens. There's an air of joviality whenever the two get together. They have known each other since Robert was a boy and they get on well. The younger man is 30 years Dave's junior and accepts that he's going to get his leg pulled, not unkindly, from time to time and he takes it all with good humour.

Dave takes out a stopwatch. Robert's no mean shearer and, just out of curiosity, Dave's going to time him. After some deliberation Robert selects a Blackface ewe and starts, cutting aside great swathes of wool with rapid sweeps of the shears. Within 50 seconds the sheep is leaping for freedom and its fleece is lying, neatly clipped, on the floor. It's just a token test, a bit of fun. Dave's enjoyed seeing Robert battling against the ticking clock. But it's a reminder of another aspect of clipping – the worldwide interest in sheep-shearing competitions.

Some of the earliest records of competitive sheep-shearing can be found in old minute books of the Royal Bath and West agricultural show, where details of the premiums awarded for a range of achievements are listed. Among the most popular events were the shearing contests. In June 1815, in the week Wellington and Blücher were defeating Napoleon at Waterloo, Abraham Ford made his way to the Bath and West Show and painstakingly clipped three sheep 'in the best style of workmanship' in one hour thirty-three minutes. Taking second prize was Thomas Tyley, whose speed was similar (one hour thirty-five minutes) but whose finish showed an 'inferior degree of excellence'. The minute books confirm an essential point: even in the days of snails-pace shearing it was the quality of the work which counted – as well as the speed.

Shearing competitions in their modern format can be traced back to 1958 when a group of young farmers from the Wairarapa district of New Zealand's North Island staged a large-scale contest at the annual agricultural and pastoral show at Masterton. It was so successful that they decided to make it a national event which they dubbed Golden Shears. The inaugural competition attracted so many spectators that the Army had to be brought in to control the crowds.

The fastest shearers acquired cult status. They included two brothers, Godfrey and Ivan Bowen, who developed a shearing style that cut out ineffective 'blows' and refined some of the techniques that had been handed down from blade shearers to machine-clippers. 'Previously,' Ivan Bowen explained, 'what shearers were guilty of was a lot of blows where you were cutting air and blows where you weren't using the full width of the comb. It didn't take long to realise there could be a better way.' The improved method came to be known as the 'Bowen style'.

In 1953 Godfrey Bowen set a world record by shearing 456 ewes in nine hours (a record later bettered by Ivan) and he was soon in demand at agricultural shows around the North Island. At one of these, a New Zealand Wool Board member saw Bowen in action and realised the potential of such an outstanding shearer as an ambassador for the wool industry. Later that year Bowen was hired as chief instructor of the NZ Wool Board's new shearing section and demonstrated his technique at shows and shearing sheds throughout the country. Before long, he was touring the world.

Dave recalls the day in the early 1950s when he got some tips from the master. 'I went to St Boswell's mart in the Borders where Godfrey Bowen was demonstrating his new technique, and a few of us had a bit of training from him. To be honest, though, I didn't keep up his method. I never really got into that way of clipping. I just use my own way. In at the neck and then down and out; then into the neck again at the other side and finish at the tail both times. In my heyday I could do one a minute no bother. I'm left-handed to start with so it comes natural. You get more even clipping with both hands than you do with one hand.'

Word of the popularity of the Golden Shears events in New Zealand spread to Britain and in 1963 Cecil Lister of R.A. Lister and Co., one of the main producers of sheep-shearing equipment in the UK, visited New Zealand to see competition shearers in action. His enthusiasm led to the first Golden Shears championships of the UK and Eire, which were held at the Bath and West Show at Swindon in 1964. Among the shearing celebrities who attended the event was Godfrey Bowen, who gave demonstrations during the show. Since then, bonds between countries putting on sheep-shearing events have strengthened. The Golden Shears World Council was founded in 1980 and it now has nine country members: Australia, New Zealand, South Africa, Norway, England, Scotland, Wales, Ireland and Northern Ireland. World championships are held every three years, alternating between the northern and the southern hemisphere. The 2005 championships will be held in Toowoomba, Australia.

As with all activities involving physical prowess, record breaking is an obsession of the world's leading shearers. They want to prove they're the quickest and the best. On July 13th, 1996, Graham McNeil set the British individual shearing record when he clipped 589 Blackface ewes in nine hours. The record stood for seven years until July 12th, 2003, when, on a hill farm in Wales, Nicky Beynon and Rhys Jones clipped 1,317 Welsh Mountain sheep in nine hours, a record for two shearers, with Beynon's total of 670 sheep setting a new individual record.

The rules governing such strenuous competitions are strict. Anyone planning to attempt a record has to apply to the British Isles Shearing Competitions Association a month beforehand. Two days before the event they must have a medical check-up and they must be insured. On the day of the record-breaking bid they usually work in five blocks. They shear from 6.00 to 8.00 and then stop for breakfast; 9.00 to 10.45 (a snack break), then

11.15 to 1.00 pm (lunch break), 2.00 to 3.45 (tea break) and 4.15 to 6.00. All the time they're clipping, the fleeces are being taken away and weighed. They must weigh at least two kilos to ensure a decent amount of wool cover on the sheep and guarantee that the event is legitimate. Once clipped, the sheep are assessed by a judge to make sure they've been properly shorn. If the shearer's going too fast and there's an accident – a sheep may get nicked by the shears and need a stitch – that animal doesn't count towards the record.

Many of the world records are held by shearers from New Zealand, where there are categories for eight-hour as well as nine-hour shearing days. It's not helpful to make comparisons with UK records because the sheep are so different. Attempts are made solo (one clipper on his own), as 2-stands (two working together), 3-stands and so on. Just as an example, for strongwool ewes, the solo record for a nine-hour day is held by Darin Forde (720 clipped on January 28th, 1997); the 2-stand record by Darin Forde and Wayne Ingram (1,335 on February 1st, 1996); and the 3-stand by Ricky Pivac, Chris Brooker and Dion Morrell (1,857 on January 23rd, 1993). For strongwool lambs the solo record is held by Rodney Sutton (839 on December 23rd, 2000); the 2-stand by Rodney Sutton and Nigel Brown (1,637 on December 23rd, 199?); and the 3-stand by Bart Hatfield, Steve Stoney and Rodney Sutton (1,933 on December 23rd, 1997); solo women Jillian Burney (541 on January 6th, 1989). All these shearers are from New Zealand.

It seems inconceivable that anyone can clip ewes more rapidly than Darin Forde's record-setting, 80-an-hour blur of clipping. Or, in the case of women shearing strongwool lambs, Jillian Burney's one-a-minute feat accomplished over a period of nine hours in 1989. But records are there to be broken, and there is a determination among shearers, back-breaking though the job may be, to push themselves to the limit.

Back at Linshiels in Northumberland's Coquet valley, records are far from the minds of the clippers as they shear their way steadily through the sheep gathered by Dave, with Scott's assistance, the day before. At last, the fire in the brazier dies, the shearing equipment is packed away, a fresh breeze starts to blow over the moors and it's time to head homeward for tea.

∽

Wheels

When people in hill farming communities are chatting about the changes they've seen in the last 30 years opinion is divided about which has been the most beneficial development. Many cite the idea of conserving bales of grass in large airtight bags as being the most useful. Pioneered by Northumberland farmer Lloyd Forster, big-bale silage has taken the worry out of haymaking for many farmers, because rather than wait for sunny weather to dry their crop, they simply cut it and wrap it in black plastic.

But while bagged silage has been a boon on hill farms where there are cattle to feed, it's the advent of the all-terrain vehicle which has brought about a seismic shift in the way sheep are managed. On their 'quad bikes', as they're ubiquitously dubbed, farmers and their shepherds can get round their flocks much more quickly. With trailers hitched to their ATVs they can take feed supplies to sheep on the hill, move ewes and lambs to better ground during lambing time and drop fencing materials off in normally inaccessible places. Most of all, they save man and dog from the wear and tear caused by striding up steep slopes. Farmers and shepherds form one of the largest groups in the queue of people waiting for hip and knee replacements. In years to come it may be their backs which suffer from a lifetime of sitting on the seat of a bike, but at least they'll be able to walk to the hospital to see a specialist because their legs won't be so worn out.

Soon after he arrived at Blindburn Stewart was provided with a two-wheel motorbike to help him cover the farm's vast expanses. A problem soon presented itself: his main sheepdog at the time couldn't stand the noise of the machine. 'She was an awful good bitch,' he recalls, 'but as soon as I started that bike up she shot right back in the kennels. She wouldn't entertain that bike at all. She'd have been all right now we've got four-wheel bikes. She'd have just jumped on the back. But the two-wheeler was a non-starter as far as she was concerned, so I didn't really use it very much for shepherding.'

Gwen also tried the two-wheel motorbike and liked it at first. Then she fell off it and her enthusiasm cooled. Six years ago the farm's first quad bike was delivered. 'To be honest, we never looked back' says Stewart. 'I don't know how people manage without them.'

Dave Baxter, a relatively recent convert to ATVs, agrees. 'The quantity of land everyone has to cover, quad bikes are the answer,' he says. 'For getting from A to B quickly there's no rival. But you can still see your sheep, if you take your time.'

The first generation of ATVs arrived on British farms in 1970. Led by Honda's all-terrain cycle, they were mostly three-wheelers, and on uneven ground they weren't as stable as they should have been. It wasn't long before they were superseded by four-wheel bikes, sales of which have risen dramatically over the last two decades. In 1993 a total of 6,000 ATVs were sold. Ten years later, annual sales topped 10,000. Ranging from the nimble 250 cc machines costing about £3,000 to 650 cc monsters which will set you back at least £7,000, they've become extremely sophisticated; at the flick of a switch drivers on most quads can change from two-wheel-drive to four-wheel-drive and from manual to automatic. A vast array of equipment is available to go with them: mowers, rollers, chain harrows, sprayers, seed broad-casters, yard brushes, snow ploughs, salt spreaders, yardscrapers, feeders and water bowsers and in many situations, they are replacing tractors. For shepherds working on exposed hills, comfort is a priority so heated handlebar grips are supplied on some models to keep hands warm on cold days. Alternatively, specially fitted muffs are popular.

However, it is not just the shepherds and hill farmers who are using ATVs, they are also increasingly being used on lowland farms and by people working in forestry, sports ground mainte-nance, equestrian activities, and horticulture.

These days on Blindburn, as on all other hill farms, the broad wheels of a quad bike have forged a network of tracks across grassy tops, over narrow bridges and through peaty bogs. Because of its speed over the ground, the machine has made the hills easier to reach. A public road connects the farm with Makendon, which is run in conjunction with Blindburn, and concerns about traffic – limited though it is – prompted Stewart to train his dogs to hop on the bike rather than run alongside it. Not that they needed much encouragement: Collies seem to love hitching a ride.

The degree to which both shepherd and dogs adapted to the ATV can be seen from one exceptional day during lambing time a couple of years ago. Just out of interest, Stewart set the trip counter to zero before he set off round the sheep early in the morning. When he finished at night, after travelling all day backwards and forwards between the farm steading and the lambing fields, it read 75 kilometres – almost 50 miles. It would have been impossible for man and dog to travel so far on foot in one day. 'When we were really stretched I could get round four hirsels in an hour and a half, make sure everything was all right, and then go back to the farm to attend to something else.'

Not everyone in the shepherding world has welcomed the rapid spread of the quad bike, however. Viv Billingham-Parkes was born and bred into the world of sheep and sheepdogs and ran her own dogs from a very early age. In 1982 she rose to fame when she competed with her Border Collie Garry in *One Man and His Dog* on television, shortly after winning a cup for Scotland at the International Sheepdog Trials at Blair Atholl.

Viv, who lives at Tweedhope in Roxburghshire, has travelled extensively throughout North America and Europe running training seminars and judging trials. She gives tuition, training and working sheepdog demonstrations. She contends that sheepdogs working with shepherds on quad bikes lack the endurance that they had in the past. 'They don't go out and gather the sheep, the quad bike gathers them. The dog's stamina isn't tested any longer, because it's got a taxi waiting for it in the shape of a quad bike.' Viv also maintains that sheep herded by a bike tend to be more flighty than those herded by a dog. 'The dog "bosses" the sheep, but a quad bike can't,' she says.

Some even argue that quad bikes have increased shepherds'

burdens. Since they can get round their sheep much more quickly, they are expected to look after bigger numbers. Former world champion sheepdog handler Raymond MacPherson puts it this way: 'Instead of one shepherd herding 500 sheep, which was adequate to get proper results from the sheep, he's getting 1,000 to 1,500 to look after. He can't under any circumstance handle 1,500 sheep by himself, so he gets a quad bike and goes round them that way. But on a motorbike you can't see all your sheep properly. The only way to do that is on foot.'

Another concern relating to the explosion in the number of quad bikes is safety. According to the Health and Safety Executive accidents at work with ATVs in agriculture and forestry over the last ten years have resulted in 17 deaths. Non-fatal accidents are not well-reported, but they're estimated to amount to more than 1,000 serious injuries per year. The causes were usually one of the following: lack of training, excessive speed, carrying a passenger, towing a heavy load or tipping on a bank, ditch, rut or bump. Often such accidents happen on a remote corner of a farm with all the consequent problems of getting help.

More than half of all ATV riders have been thrown off their machines at some time, and with no cab or rollbar, the only protection they have is what they wear. But, although four out of five ATV fatalities in the last two years have involved head injuries, users of these bikes are often reluctant to wear helmets.

The HSE is heavily involved in campaigns to promote a better awareness of the risks of using quad bikes. So versatile are these machines that there's no prospect of them ever losing their appeal, but going on a training course to learn how to use one safely does seem to make sense.

❧

The Army Ranges

The shepherds featured in this book herd their sheep over all sorts of different terrain. But they have one thing in common: their sheep have to share their land with warlike, rather than pastoral, people. That's because the Northumberland moors they live on are part of an Army training ground. In fact, it's the largest single firing range in the United Kingdom.

The Otterburn Training Area – one of 12 in the UK – covers a massive 57,000 acres. Its 31 farms include Blindburn and Makendon, tenanted by Gwen and Stewart's employer Judith Ridley, and Linshiels, which is rented by the Carruthers family and shepherded by Dave Baxter.

It can be a challenge tending sheep on expanses of moor where infantry units are undergoing fire-and-manoeuvre training with the support of artillery, mortars, guided missiles and air-to-ground attack aircraft. Accordingly, shepherds whose flocks are, from time to time, literally in the firing line have to maintain close contact with the Army to find out when to move them. That said, they have had almost a hundred years to build up an understanding with the military and a good relationship exists between the two.

A new book called *Then and Now* written by Lt. Col. Richard Cross, OBE, formerly range commandant at Otterburn, and local historian Beryl Charlton, outlines the history of the Otterburn Ranges and traces the links that residents of the area have developed with 'The Camp'. Local people are proud to boast that no less a person than Winston Churchill conceived the idea of turning part of Upper Redesdale into an artillery practice camp.

Churchill regularly went shooting with the Northumberland aristocracy and one weekend in 1900 he was a guest at Birdhopecraig Hall near Otterburn, the shooting lodge of Lord Redesdale. Things weren't going well: the weather was foul and the birds elusive. As he gazed out over the vast tracts of moorland Churchill ventured the opinion that it would be more usefully used for artillery. As a result of this throw-away remark, Redesdale was noted as a possible site for a new range. But it was another eleven years before it became a reality.

In 1908 Richard Haldane, Secretary of State for War, created the Territorial Force, forerunner of the modern Territorial Army, by amalgamating a variety of local military organisations, some of which had been in existence for hundreds of years. Haldane was aware of the threat of a war in Europe and realised that the reserve system for the British Army needed overhauling. By 1912, his reforms had resulted in the recruitment of more than 260,000 Territorial Force soldiers.

The newly-formed force was organised and equipped in the same way as the Regular Army but was based territorially so that local soldiers could train together in local units. The growing likelihood that this new band of volunteers would be deployed abroad brought about a change of strategy from 'fortress' artillery to field artillery. The batteries of the Territorial Army were equipped with field guns towed by horses and soldiers needed extensive training facilities, including firing ranges, where they could practice. An annual two-week period of intensive training was introduced and this has remained central to the training of TA volunteers ever since.

The initial purchases for the Royal Artillery Practice Camp were made in 1911 when 17 holdings totalling 19,000 acres were acquired by the Ministry of War. The list reads like a roll-call of historic Northumberland farms. Most of them were large hill units famed for their Blackface and Cheviot sheep stock, a reputation many have proudly sustained to this day. Makendon and the part of Blindburn which lies south of the River Coquet were on the list, together with Carshope, Fulhope, Ridlees, Linshiels, West Wilkwood, Bygate Hall, Quickeningcote, Featherwood, Tofthouse, Windyhaugh, Pity Me, Bellshiel, Birdhopecraig, Stewartshiels and Silloans. Birdhopecraig Lodge was bought from Lord Redesdale for use as an officers' mess. Junior officers and other ranks were billeted in bell tents and horses were housed in wooden stables. The range's opening ceremony was held at Easter in 1911.

How shepherds fared in the change of ownership is not recorded, but many of the farms had belonged to individuals rather than large estates and they continued to farm the same land, only now as tenants of the War Office. It's presumed that, on the whole, they retained their former employees as they adapted to farming on a firing range.

Meanwhile, soldiers of the Territorial Force began to arrive at Otterburn for their 14 days of training. The men came by special train to West Woodburn and marched the ten miles to their base at Rochester to begin their fortnight of learning to fire guns. The outbreak of war in 1914 saw the start of a period of intense activity for both artillery and infantry. Trenches cut in the boggy ground a mile north of Silloans Farm provided training for soldiers due to join the fighting in France.

By the time the Second World War began guns were getting bigger and their range even greater. More land was needed and a new camp was built at Otterburn and the area covered by the ranges trebled with the purchase or requisition of more of the area's well-known farms. They included: Branshaw, North Yardhope, Cottonshope, Cottonshope Head, Shillmoor, Wholehope, Bellshiel, The Trows, Linbriggs, Potts Durtrees, Yatesfield, Headshope, Barrowburn, Lounges Knowe, Rowhope, West and East Wilkwood, Harbottle Crags, South Yardhope, Dudlees, Stewartshields and High Carrick. Land was also bought at Huel Kirk, Laingshill, Girsonfield Moor, Davyshiel Common, Carlcroft, Dunns and Wainford Rigg. These farms totalled 32,000 acres.

A new road from Low Byrness to Cottonshope was built by Italian and German prisoners-of-war who, it's claimed, supplemented their rations by dabbling in a spot of sheep rustling. It sounds an unlikely tale, but they apparently used their yodelling skills to warn of any approaching shepherds.

The return of peace at the end of the Second World War did not halt expansion at Otterburn and between 1951 and 1954 the War Office bought a further 5,100 acres of land on the southern edge of the training area including the farms The Craig, Laingshill, Dunns, Raw, High Shaw, part of Colwell Hill and Girsonfield, Barrow, Angryhaugh (where Dave Baxter lives), Holystone Common, Grasslees, Wood Houses, Herdlaw Farm, Herdlaw House and land at Hollin Burn.

In 1987, the Ministry of Defence, as it became known, added four more chunks of land at Stewartshiels Plantation, Shepherds Crag, Byrness Hill and Cold Town. The training area is now 92 square miles. The block of land to the south of the Coquet is the live firing area and is closed to the public for most of the year. To the north is a 'dry' training area used by troops on manoeuvres and is accessible along public rights of way.

The system under which farming and firing co-exist has evolved over the last 93 years. The live firing area is divided into two, the

Redesdale impact area and the Otterburn impact area. Every shot, shell or splinter must fall in these zones. And every farm within them has land outside to which stock can be shifted when firing is planned. A land warden mails details of Army firing plans to farms which will be affected. Firing times are 10 am to 4 pm in winter and 9 am to 5 pm in summer, leaving two hours of daylight at either end of the day for normal farming activities to take place. If farmers or their shepherds need guidance they speak to Range Control.

Only at lambing time does the Army beat a retreat. Except in times of national emergency (the last occasion was the Falklands War) and all firing ceases from April 15 to May 15 so that ewes may lamb in peace.

'It's a healthy relationship between farmers, shepherds and the range staff,' says Col. Cross, who was range commandant from 1986 until his retirement from the Army in 1991, and then, recruited back into active service, range officer from 1991 to 2001. 'Farming on Army ranges isn't easy. There are always going to be stresses and strains, but there are benefits too. It's preserved a very large resource brimming with wildlife and archaeological sites, because over the years the Army has encouraged the low-intensity methods of farming which are now back in fashion.'

Because the farms they shepherd are to the north of the most active area on the ranges, neither Dave, Stewart nor Gwen are conscious of there being much disturbance from the military. Occasionally they pass groups of soldiers in camouflage as they take part in exercises on the 'dry' training area, where blanks are fired. But most of the time all they are aware of is the occasional growl of guns in the distance.

8 Autumn

The Sheep Sales

In the backend to the mart they'll gan, if the prices they are dear
To celebrate they'll treat their pals to a whisky or a beer
But if the prices are bad it takes more than a drop to cheer
The cannie shepherd laddies of the hills

As the sheep population of Britain grew in the 18th and 19th centuries sheep 'fairs' sprang up on the outskirts of towns throughout the country where the farmers who bred sheep met the people who wanted to buy them. They were like today's auction sales and agricultural shows rolled into one. Tents were erected to shelter stall-holders from bad weather, and the sheep were held in a vast array of pens as they waited to come under the auctioneer's gavel.

Describing a Downland sheep fair on a damp and windy September day at the end of the 19th century the author Adelaide Gosset observed: 'There are thousands of sheep, all standing with their heads uphill. At the corner of each pen the shepherd plants his crook upright. Some of them have long brown handles, and these are of hazel with the bark on; others are of ash, and one of willow. At the corners, too, just outside, collie dogs are chained, and in addition there is a whole row of dogs fastened to the tent pegs.'

Children who accompanied their parents to sheep fairs had the opportunity to play on roundabouts and swings while the adults took part in tug-of-war contests and obstacle races, or tried out their shooting skills at rifle galleries. From the taps of barrels resting on trestle tables innkeepers poured jugs of beer to satisfy the continuous stream of thirsty shepherds, and there were booths selling scones, cakes and gingerbread. A whole range of different smells, some more agricultural than others, permeated the atmosphere and conditions underfoot were often slippery with sheep's urine seeping from the pens. All the time, the sounds of dogs barking and sheep bleating punctuated the general hubbub.

Auction marts erected on permanent sites in country towns gradually replaced sheep fairs a century and a half ago, but many of the customs established at those fairs remain the same today. For sheep farmers and shepherds, the traditional autumn sales at marts are the high point of the year. The sales provide a stage on which their carefully-groomed animals can parade before a crowd of potential buyers while an auctioneer energetically tries to sell them to the highest bidder. The 'willing buyer/willing seller' auction system is a true test of the value of livestock, and although they fervently hope that their sheep will attract spirited bidding, farmers also accept that prices are very much ruled by market trends. It isn't necessarily the auctioneer's fault if there's a 'poor trade'. Factors influencing the sheep industry across Europe can play a part.

The tradition of selling in the autumn stems partly from the need to clear hill farms of surplus sheep before the cold weather sets in. On many upland farms there's only a limited amount of in-bye land and no scope to make extra hay or silage to keep animals other than breeding stock going through the winter months. In any case, it's part of the natural order of things, as farmers and their staff prepare the way for a new cycle to begin with the start of tupping time in November.

The picturesque Northumberland village of Bellingham has grown up beside the Hareshaw burn near its confluence with the North Tyne River. Mining and agriculture were the mainstays of the local economy in the early 19th century and hiring days for shepherds and other farm servants, male and female, were held in the market place on the 13th of May, the day when tenant farms traditionally changed hands and farm labourers went looking for jobs.

For hill shepherds May was a logical time for a change-over, since it gave them almost a year in their new job before facing the ardours of lambing. During that time they could acquaint them-selves with their new flock, and get to grips with the layout of the farm and its system of marking different groups of sheep. The May Day hiring tradition has all but vanished now, but there are those who regret its passing.

In 1861 the people of Bellingham petitioned the local landowner, the Duke of Northumberland, to allow sales of wool and sheep to take place three times a year in the village. The Duke gave his assent, and within a few years a mart was opened. Its proprietors were William and Thomas Taylor Iveson, auctioneers from Hawes in North Yorkshire, who also ran a mart on what is now Beaumont Street in Hexham, 20 miles away. The Ivesons were soon to merge with a business run by another Hexham auctioneer, William Cook, and together they opened a new mart at Maiden's Walk, on the other side of the market town.

The company's Bellingham mart, located in the centre of the village, had two sale rings. Ring Number One, which is still in use today, was typical of timber buildings of its type. Its centre was open to the elements but there was cover for the auctioneer and farmers perched on a circle of benches round the ring. Number Two was a small, open-air ring made from hurdles with the auctioneer's rostrum in one corner. It was replaced at the end of the Second World War by a wooden mart from the nearby village of Wark, which had been used as a government-controlled live-stock grading centre during the war. It is also still in use.

With the two rings selling sheep simultaneously, throughput can be considerable at busy times. At one sale in the early 1960s a total of 21,000 sheep were sold in one day. The office staff worked through the night to make sure payments were ready for posting by 5 am the following morning. One farmer called in to thank the mart staff on the second day of the sale, saying he had sold his sheep at 7 pm the previous evening and received his cheque on his breakfast table at 7 am the next morning. In the days when computers weren't even dreamed of and every transaction was still processed by hand that was some achievement.

Many auction marts in outlying places have closed in the last half century but Bellingham has hung on. The first Friday in October is, by tradition, the date when the owners, Hexham and Northern Marts, hold their main Blackface sheep sale at the centre. It's one of just two sales still held at Bellingham. Nevertheless, more than 10,000 sheep are on offer and staff know it will take about six hours to bring them all under the hammer.

On the stroke of 10.30 a clerk emerges from the mart office and vigorously rings a hand-bell. To many former pupils of village schools – and there will be plenty of those at Bellingham today – it evokes memories of the playground and the sound of the bell which tolled the end of break. But here it's a signal that the clatter of commerce is about to begin as the auctioneers plug in their microphones and launch into selling.

No seller wants to be first into the ring before all the buyers have arrived. Neither are they keen on being last when buyers have completed their purchases and are getting ready to go. So the auction company holds a ballot. A list of the entries is drawn up as they come in and, a week before the sale, lots are drawn to decide where on the list selling should begin. It's a fair system and a disappointing 'turn' one year may be followed by a good one the next.

The first lot in Ring One is 40 Blackface draft ewes from Ridlees Craigshield. As auctioneer Trevor Simpson gets to work, his quickly fire delivery drawing bids from all sides, the vendor stands in front of the rostrum proudly watching his carefully-prepared sheep parade around the ring. In his mind he has the figure he's expecting to get, and he urges Trevor to keep seeking bids. The auctioneer will do his best. Marked on his catalogue is who bought these sheep last year and how much they paid. 'A lot of people buy the same ewes off the same place year after year,' Trevor explains. 'They find that the sheep do well for them and they keep coming back. So you know at least one person to look for to get a bid.'

Conditions are perfect for the sale with a cloudless blue sky, no wind and not a hint of rain. Stretched out as far as the eye can see over a grassy field are pens made up from wooden hurdles.

Farmers and shepherds grip their specially carved mart sticks, giving reluctant sheep an occasional prod. Mart staff, making rustling noises with empty plastic fertiliser bags, gently chivvy ewes down corridors towards the sale rings. In the canteen, cooks are unpacking rolls fresh from the local bakery, warming soup, and heating up pies.

It's always been the tradition for sheep to be listed in the catalogue under the name of the farm they come from: Horseholme, Scrainwood, Shirlawhope, Sewingshields, Briaredge. No name of farmer, no full address, it's just assumed that people will know where the farm is and who runs it. And certainly to everyone at the sale, from the boy coaxing a dozen lambs into a pen to the grizzled old shepherd who's getting out from under his wife's feet for the day, that name will conjure up a string of associations. Maybe in their minds they can picture the farm and the surrounding land, and how exposed – or how sheltered – it is in winter. They've almost certainly known the farmers and shepherds who worked on that farm in the past – and probably who they married as well! Perhaps they remember the prizes the sheep won at local shows over the years. Possibly they can even recall the price sheep from that farm made at the same sale last year, and the year before. For, like the auctioneer, many keep the catalogues from sales in the past, carefully marked with prices, and these records of transactions which have taken place over decades are pored over at firesides on winter nights, in the same way that race-goers will study the form of horses entered for the next day's races.

Some lots are listed not just under the name of the farm, but also the hirsel: Linhope Out Bye, Featherwood North Hope. This indicates the exact part of what is a very large farm those sheep are from, and it's a guide to buyers who have bought animals from those hirsels in the past that stock from the same piece of ground are on offer.

The dream of every seller is to 'top the mart' by getting the best price in the section of the sale they have entered. It's not only the financial reward, it's a question of pride. A fierce spirit of competition exists between sheep breeders, be they farmers or shepherds. They want to be the best, and a great deal of effort will go into making their animals look the best on the day. Having selected a batch of around ten or twenty of their best sheep (known as the first 'draw') they'll dip them and then remove unwanted wool from round the neck and ears before gently trimming the fleece with a pair of shears. The objective is to make the whole bunch look as even as possible, while still emphasising qualities that will induce a buyer to write a big cheque.

Aside from those attending the sale, who else will know that a farm's Mule gimmers or Blackface ewe lambs have topped the sale? The whole farming community will, once they settle down to scan the farming page in their local newspaper. For listed there, in another tradition begun back in the 19th century, are the farms whose sheep commanded the best prices. It's a confirmation of their achievement, and, in a small way, an advertisement for their stock. Fifty years ago, almost every farm represented at a sale received a mention. But today, papers devote fewer column inches to agriculture and the farm names in many mart reports fall prey to the delete button on the sub-editor's keyboard. Auction companies complain bitterly, and no wonder. Another traditional aspect of their business is being eroded.

Lot 37 is a consignment of 60 Blackface draft ewes from The Dunns, where Robert McKay is shepherd. These are ewes that have completed their years on a hill farm but are still considered healthy enough to have one last crop of lambs in the comparative comfort of a lowland sheep unit. Awaiting his turn, Robert freshens up the six-year-old ewes' mottled faces and horns with a wipe of a rag soaked in vegetable oil. 'It puts a bit of shine on their faces,' says Dave Baxter, who's come to the sale to help the younger shepherd. 'Makes them look healthy.'

Robert's split his ewes into two groups of 30. He follows them into the auction ring, with Dave and another shepherd trailing in his wake, and starts to send the sheep round in a continuous river of grey wool. Soon there's a blur of movement with Dave, the hub, rotating in the centre and shushing the sheep while the animals circle anti-clockwise round him and Robert and another shepherd walking clockwise on the outside facing the sheep as they mill round. The skills of the three shepherds combine to show off the sheep to their best advantage. The whole picture has an almost mesmerising quality, resembling a carousel of man and beast as the bids go up and up. After less than a minute the bidding stops and the hammer comes down. The ewes have made a very acceptable £59 a head. They haven't quite topped the mart, but they'll be listed in the newspaper mart reports as one of the best of the day.

'That was the way I was taught to show off your sheep in the auction ring,' says Dave. 'The idea is you can see the sheep individually during the time they're in the ring. Draft ewes are usually sold in lots of 50, but if you put 50 sheep in the ring in a big heap they just seem to smother up to one another and nobody can see what they're like. That's why we send them round and round. It's about displaying the good qualities of the sheep. It's not a question of hiding faults. If there's anything wrong with them they shouldn't be there. Besides, if the buyers get them home and find a fault they're not going to come back to buy sheep off you next year, and then you've killed the goose that laid the golden egg.'

'Stand on! Stand on!' As Robert's second lot of draft ewes file into the ring Trevor Simpson tries to start them at the price the previous pen finished at. It doesn't always work, despite the auctioneer's urgings to 'stand on'. Buyers have minds of their own and they'll start the bidding at the lowest possible point they can.

Autumn is Dave's favourite time of the year. 'I like the autumn sheep sales,' he says. 'You get a bit of action, and you see everyone. It's sociable.' He's been coming to Bellingham since 1958. He approves of the traditional way they do things at the sale. 'The grass pens are better than concrete,' he says, 'because the muck and the water from the sheep disappear and they stay clean.' He also has views about penning sheep prior to selling them. 'You don't want too many sheep in a pen because they start to jump on one another and all the work you spent dipping and clipping them is wasted. Make sure they've got room, so that their coats don't get what we call "clapped together" – all squeezed up.'

These days, all the sheep at the sale arrive and depart in livestock transporters, but it's not so many years since they were all driven on foot to the autumn sales. Most country people welcomed the practice. They weren't in such a rush in those times – and in any case, it's supposed to be lucky to meet a flock of sheep on the highway. 'I can remember an old sheepdog handler, Davey Dickson, who lived near Hawick in Roxburghshire, he used to walk his sheep to the mart in Hawick, driving them through the streets like the drovers did in the old days. Us boys used to give him a hand with them. We'd stand at street corners and turn them into the mart for him. There was a big sale at Rothbury in Northumberland in those days and I've seen thousands of sheep flocking into the town, driven on foot by shepherds and dogs. Then they closed that sale and moved it from Rothbury to Bellingham.'

There's a note of regret in Dave's voice. The sheep sales at Rothbury, a market town slightly bigger than Bellingham, were an excuse for shepherds to really let their hair down. Many of the sheep in the early days were Cheviots from farms over the Scottish border and for the shepherds on those farms it was like a week's holiday. The sheep were driven on foot for 15 miles to stay overnight at a friend's farm, where the bottles were no doubt lined up on the kitchen table in anticipation of getting the spirits to really flow. Next day they were walked to the outskirts of Rothbury, where they were penned in a series of walled enclosures. The following day, 'dressed' (groomed) for the sale, they were escorted to the mart through the town's streets. On the fourth day, the shepherds would gingerly make their way home, nursing heavy hangovers. The Turk's Head Hotel was their favourite watering hole, and not just because it had an all-day licence. In the back room customers were able to buy platefuls of the best home-made food: thick slices of ham from huge joints, mutton pie and roast beef.

Some of the older visitors to Bellingham mart can remember the rows of sheepdogs tied to a fence next to the ring. While shepherds sold their master's sheep, it was either a case of leave the dogs by the fence or tie them up in the buildings of a farm in the village. The farm's owner understood dogs and was happy to let them do this, so long as the collie wasn't a bitch in season, otherwise all the village dogs would gather round like wasps on a jam jar and there'd be a cacophony of yapping and snarling.

A network of rural railways served the farming community well from the late 1800s to the middle of the 20th century. Many of the sheep bought at sales at Bellingham were walked the short distance to the town's station and loaded onto trucks to be drawn by steam locomotives down the North Tyne valley line to Hexham and thence to places further afield. These sheep would be set free from the trucks by their new owners at stops all over the country and turned into fields to begin a fresh stage in their lives, far from the harsh conditions of the Northumberland hills in winter. But even that mode of transport was forced to come to an end in 1956 when the North Tyne line was closed, and the sound of sheep thronging round Bellingham station was silenced for ever.

After dinner, Gwen and Stewart make an appearance at the sale. They've taken the afternoon off to check how 'the trade' is going and catch up with friends and family. 'I thoroughly enjoy it,' says Stewart. 'It's an opportunity to meet people you maybe haven't seen since the same sale a year ago. You get a good crack with your mates and you see what price the sheep are making. At the end of the day what you're striving for is to produce as good a lamb as you can and hopefully sell for the best price you can get. There's a lot of competition to do well, and the mart is your showcase.'

Two of Stewart's brothers, who live near Bellingham, have entered Blackface ewe lambs for the sale. Gwen goes into the ring to help them show off the sheep, tapping her stick on the sawdust as she makes them go round. 'Anyone we know we'll give them a hand,' Stewart says. 'I know fine well if I was selling lambs and asked them for assistance they would drop everything and help me. That's the way it works in the farming community.'

❧

Gathering the Hills

They climb out 'mong the heather ere it's turned the break of day
Cross the peat, the bent, the moss-haggs and the bogs they'll wend
*   their way*
Quick to catch a ewe that's marked or a tup that's strayed away
That's the canny shepherd laddies of the hills.

It's 7 am on a chilly Monday in late autumn. At the exposed head of the Coquet valley autumn has arrived. The beech trees protecting the eastern side of Blindburn farmhouse are copper-coloured and the bracken, which spreads like a stain over the lower parts of the hills, is turning from green to brown. A thin mist clings to the tops like a scarf. The road through the farm is wet from a shower which fell earlier in the day.

For most of their lives hill sheep remain on their own ground, but on a number of important occasions in the year they have to be rounded up and brought down to the farm. These 'gathers' are carried out in order to inject ewes before lambing, castrate and mark lambs after lambing, clip the ewes, wean the lambs, and sort sheep before tupping time. We've come to film this practice on an October day which the forecasters said would be clear and dry. Not for the first time, they've got it slightly wrong and a distinct lack of visibility is holding things up. The land on Blindburn rises to over 1,600 feet (510 metres) and on a day like this low cloud can pose problems.

But there's a country saying:

Rain before seven

Fine before eleven

And at last, after innumerable discussions about the reliability of weather forecasts and much squinting at the distant peaks, the decision is made. The round-up will take place, mist notwithstanding. Stewart and Matthew roar off on their quad bikes, dogs sitting behind them, to gather the sheep from two of the farm's outlying hills. Meanwhile, Gwen sets off on foot accompanied by her collie, Jill, and two other dogs.

The cameraman and I look at the hill behind the farmhouse. There's only one word for it: steep. He's quite a few years younger than me, and he's also someone who goes to the gym twice a week. My exercise consists of walking down to the newsagents from time to time to pick up a paper. We've a camera, tripod and bag to carry, and (unlike the shepherds) we don't have sticks. But there's no way round it. If we want to film sheep being gathered off the Cheviots, we'll just have to get going. Fortunately, as we climb out of the valley, a track appears in front of us, snaking its way to the top of the first fell, and before long we are looking back at the water tumbling down the Coquet far below. Wheelmarks in the mud show that this is the route taken by Stewart and Matt on their ATVs. There are few landmarks to guide us but we can tell we're on the right track.

The plan is to rendezvous at a ruined farmhouse which lies north of Blindburn, half-way to the Border. It's out of sight below the crest of a distant hill at the moment but the track worn by the bikes can be clearly seen as it zig-zags across the grassy slope towards the horizon. These are the desolate areas where we might spot groups of the wild goats that roam the Cheviot Hills, but they're keeping a low profile today.

Although it's now part of Blindburn, Yearning Hall, the ruin we are heading towards, was once a farm in its own right. A photograph of it, taken at the beginning of the 20th century, shows a single-storey, slate-roofed house with a small porch, a cow byre and a black corrugated-iron lean-to. The building faces south, and in front of it is a small clump of thorn bushes and a fenced-off vegetable patch. Adjoining this is a paddock where a house cow, its head down, is grazing contentedly. At the foot of the paddock there's a tin-roofed hen-house, and a dog's kennel, also made from corrugated iron, stands next to the house. Round the back there would probably have been a pigsty and a spring to draw water from. There must also have been an outdoor 'netty' (earth closet) but there is no sign of it in the picture.

Almost certainly there would have been a pile of peats next to the back door since this was the main fuel burned in farmhouse grates in those days. The right to dig peat is known as 'turbary' and it was exercised by the families of farmers and shepherds in the Cheviots until quite recently, as it was in upland areas all over Britain. The peats were cut in June, when the moors were at their driest. The main tool was a V-shaped peat spade not unlike the hay spades used to cut slices of hay from haystacks. Wives and children, who always assisted at the peat-digging, had the job of laying the black peats flat on the heather to allow the moisture to seep out. After a month they would be set up, like bricks on end, to continue to dry in the sun and wind. A few weeks later, the peats were collected by horse and cart and transported back to the farm. It was reckoned a family needed 40 cartloads of peat to keep them going through the winter, so the peat stack was often higher than the house itself.

Smoke is spiralling from one of the two chimneys jutting

from the roof and one can imagine the farmer's wife stoking the fire as she prepared a meal for her husband and the shepherds, who would soon be returning from 'looking' the sheep. They were virtually self-sufficient in food, although other basic requisites would have to be fetched, sometimes by pony but more often on foot, from Barrowburn, several miles away, where forerunners of today's farmers' markets were held. Carriers from towns further afield would venture up the valley to meet the inhabitants and barter goods such as flour, sugar, salt, oatmeal and tea for the butter, eggs, rabbits and hens that the shepherds' families brought. It was a hard life, little more than an existence.

The biggest surprise in the photograph of Yearning Hall is a pair of haystacks standing on level ground behind the house. To make hay you needed a decent selection of horse-drawn tackle: reaper, turner, buckrake, sweep and bogey (low-level trailer). How they brought them across the moors is a mystery, but there must have been a track of sorts, even if today there are no obvious signs of it.

Having enough help to make hay, however, was not a problem, as can be gathered from the census of 1841. It gives an intriguing insight into how densely the area now covered by Blindburn was populated. It also indicates how people earned a living, because for the first time, the census lists people's occupations. At Makendon there were four people: two shepherds, a woman and a child. At Buckham's Walls (now also a ruin) there were eight people, only one of whom was a shepherd. At Yearning Hall the seven inhabitants were the farmer, his wife and three children, together with two shepherds. And at Blindburn itself the 15 people comprised the farmer, his wife, three shepherds, a retired shepherd aged 80, five children and six farm servants, male and female. That's 34 people. Today there are just five.

As for Yearning Hall, it's just a shell. The roof has caved in and the walls are crumbling. You can see where the fireplace stood, but there are few other signs of human habitation. The families that lived there are long gone.

As we stand gazing at the ruin, low cloud drifts across the landscape and the surrounding hills slip in and out of view. But soon we can hear the sound of barking and Gwen appears, her dogs behind her. From a vantage point overlooking the valley of the Blind Burn, a tributary of the Coquet far below us, she has been looking out for signs of sheep being gathered. Almost at once we pick up the buzz of the quad bikes and sheep start to leave the far-off hillsides, flowing down sheep tracks like a white river, with Stewart and Matt's dogs at their heels. The cameraman starts filming. What he's recording is an exhibition of skill as men and dogs combine to flush out several hundred sheep and direct them back to the farm. True, they have their quad bikes to help them, but that apart, this is a timeless scene. 'What you need when you're gathering sheep in an area like this is a dog that will think for itself,' says Stewart. 'A lot of the time my dog's working out of sight and I'm trusting it not to miss any sheep'. He laughs good-naturedly. 'Well, that's the theory anyway. Sheep being sheep, it doesn't always happen that way!'

Sheepdog-handler Derek Scrimgeour, the author of *Talking Sheepdogs*, a guide to training collies which is mentioned elsewhere in this book, has this advice on gathering from steep accessible fells:

Your dog needs to be patient. Give the sheep time on the mountain, time to make their own decisions rather than run into

problems. There's a place for a sheep to be and a route for it to go.
If they don't decide for themselves exert a little pressure, and then
relax a bit and let nature take its course. Things I used to rush at
as a youngster I take more time with now.

Judith has walked up the Blind Burn valley to meet the sheep
coming off the hills. She and Gwen take over the herding and
start to drive the flock back down the side of the burn while
Stewart and Matt remain on the hilltops, eyes peeled for the odd
stray sheep. At one point, Stewart, patrolling the other side of the
valley, spots three ewes in the heather way above Gwen. They are
plainly reluctant to join the general throng, but because of the
sharp angle of the valley side, she can't see them. With a mobile
phone, he would be able to alert her, but you can't get a signal in
this part of the country, so Stewart has to resort to shouting.
There follows a brief moment of marital misunderstanding with
Gwen unable to make out what her husband's hollering about.
When eventually she grasps what he's saying and dispatches Jill
to round up the elusive trio, the dog can't see them either and
ends up missing them. Watching from the other side of the
valley, Stewart shakes his head in frustration. Being a Collie,
however, Jill's not one to give up easily. She lopes up the steep
incline again and this time spots the strays. They immediately get
the message and trot down to join their colleagues as if nothing
had happened.

Gwen says that, working together, she and Stewart have become
quite intuitive. 'We do argue now and again,' she says, laughing.
'But who doesn't? The rest of the time we get on. We like being
together. There can't be many husbands and wives who work
together in such close proximity and get on as well as we do.'

The cameraman wants to get ahead of the sheep so that he can film them as they emerge from the valley. It's another classic shot, but by this stage the flock is moving at a steady pace. If we're to outflank them, we'll need to do some rapid yomping through peaty burns and waist-high rushes. By the time we get where we want to be the camera bag is starting to feel very heavy indeed and it's beginning to dawn on me why the Army use the area for training soldiers!

∿

The Shepherds' Show

Arguments, often bitter ones, were what ignited the spark for a shepherds' show up in the Cheviot Hills more than 150 years ago. Then, as now, sheep men had strong opinions. Disputes would break out over whose was the best Cheviot ewe, or which flock produced the bonniest Blackface lambs. Men's pride was at stake and the only way to settle matters was to get sheep and shepherds together before an independent judge and let him decide. Not that anyone ever agrees with his decision; there are always dissenters and judging any competition is a lonely, some say thankless, task – you please no one but yourself. There's a story that at one of the early shows a shepherd was aggrieved that the judge had awarded first prize for Blackface ewes to one of his arch rival's sheep. The shepherd cornered the judge, demanding to know what he had against his ewe. 'Nowt,' replied the judge. 'I just liked t'other yin better!'

Once the judging was over, shepherds could get down to the real business of the day – having a wee dram or two and eventually they would return to their farms in isolated parts of the Cheviot Hills, content in the knowledge that the merits of their animals had been recognised. Moreover, some of them had received a prize to prove it.

The early shows were held on farms in the hills. Kidlandlee is one settlement where shows were held in the 1830s and 1840s. It's believed that only Cheviot sheep were allowed to be shown in the early years and it was some time before Blackface sheep were also considered worthy enough to take part. By 1850 the show had settled at Alwinton Village where a level area of low-lying land (called the haugh) is conveniently situated beside the road. It's an ideal site and the show has been held there every year except in times of war or after outbreaks of foot and mouth disease.

The winds blowing up Northumberland's remote Coquet Valley were so strong that some exhibitors found it difficult to put up their marquees. But by dawn the next morning a calm had descended over the showground and the remaining tents were erected without any problems, the sun warming the backs of the marquee men as it rose over the hills to the east.

The Border Shepherds Show at Alwinton is the last agricultural show of the year. Held on the second Saturday in October, it isn't usually blessed with fine weather. But 2003 is an exception: it's so warm that visitors are strolling around the show field in shirt sleeves. There's even a report of someone fainting from the heat, not a common occurrence in this normally draughty corner of Northumberland in late autumn. Summoned to attend, the air ambulance helicopter buzzes its way up the valley and lands in the tiny ring where the dog show is about to take place. It's soon on its way back to Newcastle's General Hospital and the show's timetable continues to amble along its pre-arranged course.

The 2003 show is in fact the 138th 'annual exhibition' where as well as sheep, there are classes for dogs, walking sticks, vegetables, flowers, jam, baking, fresh eggs, dyed eggs, sloe gin, home-made lemonade, home-made ginger wine, knitting, oil paintings, water-colours and photographs. To ensure there are competitors in the future, there's also a section for children with categories for writing, painting, baking and craftwork.

Gwen, wicker basket on arm, bustles along the avenue between the marquees and the stalls selling outdoor clothing. She's heading for the tent where long trestles draped in white are start-ing to groan under the weight of Coquetdale cooking at its most substantial. The non-farming part of the show is called the 'industrial' section for reasons that are not immediately clear, except to say that it seems to have been organised on an indus-trial scale. Tables are laid out end to end, covered with an assortment of food that would keep a gang of sheep-shearers quiet for several weeks: meat pasties, savoury flans, cheese scones, bacon-and-egg pies, bread, teacake, currant scones. dropped scones, brown scones, girdle scones, granny loaves, apple pies, tea loaves, sausage rolls, chutney, jelly, raspberry jam, blackcurrant jam, strawberry jam, lemon curd and marmalade – and that's just the 'plain baking'. A huge spread of 'fancy' baking fills the rest of the tent: ginger bread, chocolate-coated biscuits, ginger snaps, rock buns, sponge cakes, cherry cakes, sandwich cakes, fruit loaves, chocolate cakes, traybakes, sultana cakes, orange cakes, coffee cakes, rice cakes, shortbread, angel cakes, truffles, caramel shortcake, date and walnut cakes, Swiss rolls, carrot cakes and queen cakes. There's even a class for 'Baking

Gone Wrong', but it's not very well subscribed. So expert are most of the entrants that their bread never fails to rise, nor do their cakes sag in the middle.

Gwen makes her way straight to the table where plain baking is being displayed. She's competing in the class for drop scones, one of several categories she's entered. On the tablecloth lie some numbers in strips, torn from a book of raffle tickets. In her show catalogue Gwen checks the number for her entry and with great care she unwraps her four scones and arranges them on a doily on the table, pinning her entry number to the paper. 'When I look at the others they're nice and round,' she sighs. 'Mine aren't anywhere near so perfect. But you never know, the judge might like them.'

There's an air of mild panic about the marquee. It's 10.25 and all exhibitors are rushing to lay out their produce. Everyone has to have finished their stands by 10.30 and the tent has to be cleared by 11, when the judging begins. The rule about judging is strict: while it's taking place no one except the secretary and the judges may remain in the tent.

Class 138 in the fancy baking category is for gingerbread. With much rustling – and a certain amount of good-natured jostling – Gwen and another competitor unwrap their entries from silver foil and arrange them on small trays. Already gracing the white tablecloth are gingerbreads as big as breeze blocks, but Gwen's optimistic: 'I felt I might stand a better chance if I entered two,' she says. 'One's a new recipe I haven't tried before so I thought I'd give it a go. I would like a prize for my gingerbread, but there are a lot of expert cooks in the area. If you win a prize at Alwinton you're doing well.'

Gwen spends about a week before the show preparing her

entries for the show in the hope of at least feeling she's done herself justice or, even better, winning something. Her four rock buns, bursting with raisins, look positively mouth-watering, but there are 18 entries in the class – a lot for the judge to taste before deciding which are the best. 'It's fun to take part,' Gwen says. 'It's competitive, but it's not too serious. I like to see the community getting together. The show takes a lot of organising and everyone has to do their bit.'

Gwen has also brought an entry for Class 162: three fresh eggs, because their free-range hens are laying well at the moment. 'The judge breaks them and assesses the yolk,' she says. 'Who knows, I might be lucky.'

The pastimes of spinning and knitting were once part of every-day life in remote hill farms in the North of England, Wales and Scotland – with only open fires for heating, everyone spent the winter wrapped in layers of warm clothing. Agricultural shows like Alwinton reflect that aspect of our rural past with classes for knitted socks, quilted articles, woollen hats, jumpers, cardigans, sweaters, jackets, embroidery, crochet, cross stitch, tapestry, pin cushions and tea cosies, not forgetting fancy, hand-spun yarn. 'I've just started knitting, so it's the first time I've entered,' explains Gwen, holding up the grey child's jumper she's just completed. 'I'm knitting for my nephews and nieces, mainly, but I suppose it is part of a tradition. I've seen shepherds knitting in the past. There was one on the farm where I was a student who used to knit his own socks. Good hardwearing socks they were too.' Could Stewart be persuaded to take up knitting needles? Gwen laughs. 'Not my husband,' she says. 'He likes a good book. Knitting is definitely not his scene.'

Once again, the rules surrounding knitwear are unequivocal.

Articles which have been entered at a previous Alwinton Show are not allowed, and 'professionals and teachers of fancy work' are debarred from competing because their expertise would give them too much of an advantage.

Outside on the showground the sound of pipes and drums wafts across the valley. The local pipe band is coming down the lane to play at the show. It's heart-stirring stuff and Gwen joins the crowd as it surges forward to the main ring where the band is about to perform.

The Rothbury Pipe Band was formed on a very auspicious day: June 31st, 1920. At least, that's what one of the band's old minute books says. The fact that June only has 30 days doesn't seem to have put anyone off; perhaps they were just trying to prolong the days of summer that year. Anyway, the band's still going strong. In its 84 years it's played at dances, flower shows and local sports. It's been the main attraction at carnivals, miners' picnics, lifeboat fêtes and agricultural shows. It's even played at a few funerals. But the band's greatest claim to fame is that it played on the hallowed turf at St James' Park, home of Newcastle United FC. In a far-off era when local bands used to entertain the fans at half time, the Rothbury Pipe Band made regular appearances at the famous ground.

However, not all their concerts were so illustrious. In September 1922, just two years after it was formed, the pipers' band broke their journey in the Tynedale village of Haydon Bridge on the way back from playing a charity concert at Alston in Cumbria, England's highest market town. Feeling a few pangs of hunger, they decided to get out the bagpipes and play for their tea.

'When we started to play there wasn't a soul on the street, but by the time we'd finished there was a very big crowd,' the minute book says. 'The people took the collection themselves, a lady going round first and a gentleman afterwards. After paying for the teas we had £1 8s 2d for the collection'.

On the stroke of midday the flaps are thrown back on the door of Alwinton Show's industrial tent to allow exhibitors to rush in and see the results of the judging. Tickets are laid on the displayed exhibits: red for first, light blue for second, yellow for third. But sadly, Gwen's hopes of picking up a prize are dashed. Well-used Agas in farmhouse kitchens in Coquetdale have turned out some high-class baking and, for this year at least, Gwen's entries aren't among the winners. Even her gingerbread fails to get a ticket.

Ever optimistic, Gwen shrugs off the disappointment: 'It was nice to daydream about getting a prize. But it wasn't to be. There are some very good cooks in this area and the standard at Alwinton is always high. But I'll be back next year to try again.'

Dave Baxter is leaning against the rails at the sheep pens, relaxing in the sunshine. He would normally be among the people showing sheep at Alwinton, but since the outbreak of foot and mouth disease in 2001 the restrictions on animal movements have deterred many – including Dave – from taking their animals to agricultural shows; there are too many forms to fill in. As it happens, two officials from Defra are visiting the show to keep a check on exhibitors' paperwork. Alwinton is not alone in being affected by the aftermath of foot and mouth. Across the country entry numbers in livestock classes at small agricultural shows are lower than they used to be, and some predict they may never recover.

However, even with the low number of entries, the competition is still fierce, just as it was when the show began in the middle of the 19th century. Moreover, the show's sheep section retains features which go back to the very beginning. Even though the number of shepherds in the Cheviots is markedly lower than it used to be there are still classes solely for shepherds. Best South Country Cheviot Sheep, Pack (from a shepherd's own small flock) or Hirsel (sheep from an area of hill which a shepherd looks after for their boss) is the description of one of the classes.

Large agricultural shows boast classes for a wide range of sheep, but a small country show like Alwinton concentrates on the breeds which are dominant in the area. True, there's a category for Jacob sheep, a once-endangered breed well-known for its black-and-white wool and imposing set of horns. But the other classes are for the stalwarts of the local farming economy: Blackface, Cheviot and Swaledale sheep. Mule sheep, got by crossing Swaledale and Blackface ewes with a more prolific Bluefaced Leicester ram, are also included.

The rules governing the sheep entries again reflect the area: all sheep must be fed on 'normal hirsel fare', which means they mustn't be given supplementary feed to boost them, and all lambs must be true hill lambs, that is, born after April 1st.

As judging time approaches, strenuous efforts are being made by farmers and shepherds to present their sheep in the best possible light. 'Just like a lady getting ready for a dance,' says one old-timer watching the care that's being taken. The animals' faces are washed and dried and fleeces, which have been endlessly trimmed back at the farm, are once more combed and patted to give them the desired shape – a shape which, it's hoped, will attract the judge's approval. The prize money is not large (£5 for first, £3 for second and £1 for third) but honour is at stake.

When Dave's showing his Blackface sheep the process starts on the Wednesday, four days before a show. The show animal will be washed in an old bath and allowed to dry naturally, before being trimmed with the shears on the Thursday. Friday will see Dave wandering along the banks by local streams in search of red and brown clay. It seems bizarre, but having washed the sheep's fleece two days previously, he's now going to colour it again with handfuls of clay. It's a special technique, one which Dave learned from elderly shepherds in his youth, and it's all part of the skill of 'bringing out' a show sheep. With their ruddy-brown fleeces, they have a certain beauty and they certainly stand out.

Dave's normally far too unsentimental to give a sheep a name. But one year he bred a Blackface ewe lamb that won practically every show he took it to, and for some reason he and Mona decided to call her Lydia. The following summer he continued to show the sheep as a 'gimmer' (one-year-old). So used was Lydia to being washed and coloured every week that she would stand patiently while it was being done. When the moment came to leave home for another day at a show, she would happily jump into the van without being prompted.

All the titivating and trimming has certainly served Dave well. He recalls one visit to Alwinton Show when his children were young. Crammed in the back of his van he had two sheep, two dogs and the pram. 'I had a really good day,' he says. 'I won the sheepdog trial and the collie dog class at the dog show, and got two first prizes with the sheep. The only disappointment was there wasn't a bonny baby contest. We might have won that too!'

For Dave, the charm of a small country show is its unchanging nature. In the days before specialised livestock transport was developed, shepherds used to drive their sheep to the agricultural shows on foot, just as they drove them across country to the autumn sheep sales. 'It was a week's job, going to Alwinton Show and coming back afterwards,' he laughs. 'They'd take two or three days to get to Alwinton, stopping at shepherds' houses on the way where there was plenty of whisky to drink and a big feed laid out on the kitchen table. They'd arrive at Alwinton the night before the show and get stuck into the drink in the pub. Next morning they'd be up at dawn to get their sheep ready for the show and when it was all over they'd set off for home on a journey which would take another two days at least. You see, those days, they didn't get away from home much. The occasional show like Alwinton and the lamb sales at Rothbury or Bellingham were the highlight of the year. Mind, they must have been hardy sheep to walk to the shows. They must have been good on their feet, because they'd have to cross some tough terrain to get there. It's different now, much simpler. You pull up with your vehicle and let your sheep out straight into the pens.'

Dave's talking about shows a hundred years ago, as told in tales handed down to him by generations of shepherds. He's glad Alwinton Show hasn't changed a great deal in his lifetime. 'When I first came it was just a few sheep and a dog trial. Now there are more attractions, like hound trials and a fell race, but things haven't altered that much. For me it's just right and it's on my doorstep. If I'm not exhibiting sheep I just walk to the show and walk home again. It's a perfect day today, which is a surprise at this time of the year. But everyone turns up to Alwinton Show, whatever the weather. There are some people who don't go to any other show, they just stick to Alwinton. They like it because it's traditional. How long will I keep going? Oh, I'll go to Alwinton Show right to the bitter end.'

On the other side of the showfield a crowd is beginning to form round the perimeter of the small ring. It's the moment for people to show their dogs. Not surprisingly, since this is a sheep farming area, there are classes for working sheepdogs, but also keenly contested are classes for two breeds of working terrier, the Jack Russell and the Border. The latter, with its otter-like head, dark eyes and keen expression, comes in a variety of colours: red, grizzle-and-tan and blue-and-tan. The Jack Russell, an alert, combative terrier, seems to be available in a variety of coats, if the entries are anything to go by.

Gwen is competing with Jill, her two-year-old bitch, in the Border Collie class, where there's a familiar face from the sheep-dog handling world. Scott Smith, from Seahouses, is parading his bitch and the judge, Matt Little, obviously likes the look of her because she's the one to receive the red ticket and £2 prize money. 'It's not like Crufts,' Gwen giggles. 'It's just a bit of fun. We have a laugh, a bit of banter. We don't handle the dogs professionally. We just walk them round the ring and let the judge decide.' Jill actually makes the shortlist of four from which the top three will be chosen, but she's out of luck. She ends up in fourth place, but there's no prize for that. 'She's a bit lean and that may have counted against her,' says Gwen. 'She's the type of dog I can't put weight on at the moment, but that'll change when she's mature. Every judge is different. Some like a rough-haired dog, some like smooth-haired. Some like black-and-white collies. Some prefer them with a bit of brown. You just have to show your dog and hope it's what they're looking for.'

Gwen has better luck in the Jack Russell class. She's entered a smooth-haired, two-year-old bitch called Fudge. 'I bred her and sold her to a friend but she comes back to Blindburn for her holidays from time to time. She's still quite young and full of life, and when she's here I like to show her'. Fudge is clearly more to Matt Little's liking. She quickly makes the shortlist and takes second place. 'He must have liked rough-haired Jack Russells because the winner had a rough coat,' Gwen says, pocketing her prize money of £1.50. 'But I was pleased Fudge got second.'

Dave decides to pause for a few moments and watch the Cumberland and Westmorland wrestling, which is taking place in one of the rings, keenly watched by devotees of this traditional sport. A game of skill and strength which always takes place on grass, it features two wrestlers grasping each other round the body in what's known as 'back-hold' style. A bout only starts when both contestants have 'got to grips' by simultaneously linking fingers behind their opponent's back. They then attempt a series of moves to gain the upper hand. The first wrestler to lose hold, or touch the ground with any part of the body except the feet, loses the bout.

This version of the sport of wrestling is believed to have originated in Cumberland and Westmorland (the two old counties that now form Cumbria) in the 1600s. In the following century it spread to Northumberland, Durham, Lancashire and Scotland. As it became more competitive, ornate belts were offered as prizes as well as increasingly large amounts of money. Big sums were wagered on bouts and match-fixing (known as barneying) became widespread. So popular was the sport that one match in Carlisle in 1900 attracted more than 12,000 spectators. But, since then, it has slowly declined as other sports have come to the fore. Few children are now taught wrestling at school, and the mainstays of the sport are a few long-standing wrestling families.

Over the years costumes worn by wrestlers have changed considerably, as materials suffered a shortage (as happened after the Second World War) or became more abundant. Even today their outfits retain a distinctive look: a pair of socks, leggings, a centre-piece (like a man's bathing costume) and a singlet or tee-shirt.

Alwinton Show is an important event for Cumberland and Westmorland wrestlers. As well as staging classes for contestants of different ages and weights, it's also the championship venue for the national under-15s competition. The prize money ranges from £20 for the winner of the boys' under-10 class to £200 for the champion heavyweight (14 stone).

On another part of the showfield a small knot of men are walking up and down carrying iron rings and looking purpose-fully at a pock-marked area of grass. From time to time there's the distinctive clinking sound of metal on metal. It's the quoits contest, another traditional pastime which still survives at Alwinton and a few other country shows in this part of England. The game involves hurling rings up and down a pitch at target pins 11 yards away. Because of the quoits ring's resemblance to the discus some believe that the sport may have had its origin in ancient Greece and that quoits were possibly flung by athletes at the first Olympiad. How they were adopted by Britons is unclear but quoits have been played here since the Middle Ages and it was considered such a dissolute game that it was outlawed in the Sporting Regulations of 1388. Related to another game once played in the back gardens of hostelries – the throwing of horse shoes at a pin – quoits have long been associated with farm workers and miners. In fact in earlier times quoits were often made in mine forges from left-over metal.

Measuring five-and-a-half inches in diameter and weighing five-and-a-half pounds quoits are certainly not Frisbees and it takes a great deal of skill to fling them so that they land over the 'hobs' or pins. Official rules governing the game appeared in 1881, having been drawn up by a committee selected from pubs in the North of England, and, with regional variations, quoits is played much the same as it was then. Shepherds still keep up the tradition with a game from time to time.

The sun's starting to set as Dave makes his way from the show-field to a flat piece of ground a quarter of a mile away. This is the venue for the Alwinton sheepdog trial, organised every year by Stewart Wallace. He's down at the holding pens releasing the Mule gimmers, three at a time. Dave settles back to watch as Gwen competes with Jill, her three-year-old, home-bred bitch. Jill sees the sheep well and has a good outrun. But she fails to hear Gwen's 'lie down' command at the top of the course and things start to go wrong. Whether it's the midges that have just come out in clouds, or the sense of freedom that they are finally feeling, the sheep gallop down the field like Olympic sprinters. Despite Jill's efforts they scoot past Gwen and steadfastly refuse to be put through the drive gates, at which point Gwen clearly feels it's better to retire gracefully. 'Jill was getting a bit hyped up and I thought it would be best if I just came off', she explains. Jill is young and keen and Gwen feels she needs to mature for another year. 'We're still learn-ing together' she says. 'It's a hobby I enjoy. I've been trialling for a number of years. Although I've won novice prizes, I haven't had much success in the open trials. But I'll keep trying. It's the only way you succeed.'

Then it's Stewart's turn with his four-year-old bitch Marie. 'I bought her five months ago and we're still getting used to each other,' he says. 'They reckon it takes six months after a dog changes hands before it's truly settled. Marie's getting better every time she comes to the trials. She's a super little dog at home; it's just taking a while for her to adjust to rounding up three sheep rather than a whole bunch. But we'll persevere, we'll get there in the end.'

Ten minutes later, recalling his run, Stewart's pleased the young dog made a good start. 'She set off reasonably well off the right hand side, maybe a bit tight, but she had a good lift and a good fetch, flanking all right, at a nice steady pace. And then on the drive away she lay down and – shall we say – forgot to get up! Eventually, we got the sheep through the gates and then there was a bit of a hiccup on the cross drive. We got through the gates again but I just couldn't get her to pen the sheep at the end. And that was that. No excuses. The sheep were spot on, the course was spot on.'

It says volumes for Stewart's amiable nature that he refuses to blame his dog. 'If anything, it was me. Really, I should encourage Marie to work more in the pens at home and get her up close to sheep, forcing them up alleyways. I reckon another winter and she'll be there or thereabouts, picking up the odd prize.'

Stewart's pleased that the sheepdog trial has gone well. It takes a lot of organising, and it's not the only activity in the Coquet valley that he's involved with. Today, though, blessed with perfect weather, it's been a pleasure to run – and compete in. 'There's always been a sheepdog trial at Alwinton Show,' he says. 'Last show of the season, last sheepdog trial. This is my 23rd year and only once, in the foot and mouth year, have I not competed. But I'm glad it's the last trial of the year. It's been a long season and I'm looking forward to having the weekends off in the winter. And the chance to work away with my dogs.'

Now they all go down to Alwinton to see the shepherds' show
And into Foreman's pub at night they never fail to go
For to sing the songs and dance about, but fight, God bless you, no
That's the canny shepherd laddies of the hills.

9 Winter

⌒

By Hook or by Crook

It's a crisp December day and the blue of the sky is overlaid by a lattice of flimsy white cloud. A sign, Dave reckons, that strong winds are coming. Six decades of living on the land have honed his weather-forecasting skills and he could well be right. There's a restlessness in the morning air and Dave's anxious to be on his way.

Underfoot, the ground is firm, a legacy of recent icy weather. The grass crunches beneath the shepherd's boots as he strides purposefully along a well-worn track beside a stream. He's heading towards a small wood in the distance. Bracken fronds, dusted with frost, line the sides of the path. Two of Dave's sheep-dogs, Nap and Scott, follow close at his heels, eager to burn off some energy.

As Dave ambles along he's aware of growth in the trees which huddle together close to the stream. It may be winter, but there's life in the earth nonetheless. The birches' silver trunks light up the countryside at this time of year. They're not the forester's favourite tree and are often dismissed as 'scrub' because of their tendency to colonise large areas of land, but Dave loves their fragile elegance and can't wait to see them come into leaf in April and May. 'It's a beautiful tree, the birch,' he says. And it's true, there's nothing finer than a clump of light-green birches standing out against a background of purple-flowering larch in spring.

The tree has its practical uses too. The old saying may have warned:

Tis unlucky to buy a broom in May
For it will sweep all luck away.

But superstitions like that didn't deter the woodsmen of days gone by. All year round they were busy making the besoms or 'witches' brooms' that were once popular for sweeping leaves. These 'broom squires', as the men were called in some parts of England, would spend the winter trimming branches from birch trees to build up a stock of broom material. It was left for a year to stiffen before being fastened round a 'shank', or handle, made from ash. Before the days of wire, willow wands were used to clamp the handle tight. 'Them old boys were good with their hands,' Dave says. 'The materials were free, and they could make just about anything out of them.'

The birches alongside the footpath being taken by Dave have tiny, grey-brown, sausage-shaped growths hanging from their skeletal twigs. These look like the droppings of some strange animal or bird, but in fact they're the tree's male catkins. It won't be until April that they expand and droop down as attractive 'lamb's tails'. Then, when a breeze shakes the trees, you'll see them produce clouds of yellow pollen that drift languorously across the landscape.

Also growing in profusion by the stream are clumps of alders, which thrive on being up to their ankles in water. The lowland swamps where they used to grow are called 'carrs', an old Norse word meaning boggy ground. But because their leaf-fall enriches the soil, it became worthwhile for farmers to clear the trees and drain the land. Many carrs are now productive arable fields. Up in the hills, however, alders are left undisturbed. There used to be a demand for their tough, water-resistant wood to make soles for clogs, but those times are long gone.

Clasped to his shoulder Dave has a small bushman's saw, its teeth newly sharpened. As he enters the wood, his eyes dart this way and that, hunting for a thicket which will yield a crop of the straight-stemmed shoots that he's after. His quarry: hazel. And the wood is full of it. If it's left uncut, hazel can produce a decent-sized trunk and grow to around ten metres in height, but it's not strictly a tree in the true sense of the word. It's more of a shrub, producing a dense mass of long, arching branches and erect shoots.

Because of its versatility hazel is still cropped in many parts of the country. Wood-workers turn it into hurdles, gardeners use it for pea sticks and bean poles, and weavers use it for baskets. In the 18th and 19th centuries hazel spars held the thatch on cottage roofs; builders also made regular use of hazel as the 'wattle' in wattle-and daub walls; and on smallholdings high in the Pennines farmers made flimsy hay feeders with hazel sticks and lengths of rope. But for Dave, and other shepherds like him, hazel's prime role is for walking sticks. He cuts expertly into the base of the bush to harvest a stick. 'Look,' he says, 'straight as a ramrod. This is a north-facing wood, you see. It gets very little sun, and these shoots are reaching for the sky so they have to grow straight.'

Both white and brown hazels grow in this particular wood. Dave says he prefers the white. It's harder and has more attractive markings. As well as the four-foot long sticks, which in due course will be 'married' to a horn handle, Dave's searching for a sucker growing from a thicker, curved branch or root. There's a perfect example in the next clump. Dave saws through the branch, taking the one-inch-thick stick and the big knuckle of stem it's growing from. It's difficult to imagine, but in the fullness of time this will make a beautiful walking stick – all of it, handle and shank, fashioned from one piece of wood.

'You can make a nice stick with a hazel block,' Dave says. 'They're not very strong because they're cross-grained to start with, but they're good for going to a dog trial with, so long as you're not rough with them. I've one I've used for donkey's years at dog trials.'

Seasoned stick-makers say the best time to cut a stick is when you see it, the implication being that if you don't, someone else will. 'I saw one once coming back from a farm,' Dave recollects. 'It was a topper and I was determined not to miss it. As soon as I got home I got the saw and went back and cut it at the roadside.' Generally, it's best to cut hazel in winter when the sap's stopped rising. Cut in the summer, hazel has a tendency to shrink.

As for length, the advice from the experts is: cut a stick longer than you need. You can always trim an inch or two off the bottom. Depending on who's going to use it, a working shepherd's crook should be about five-feet long. A walking stick to be used as support is naturally shorter. As a rough guide, its crown (the top) should be level with the hip bone of the user.

'There's a lot of good hazel in woods in the Lake District,' Dave says. 'Dark, damp places where they can grow really straight. A chap used to come from the area near Grange-over-Sands in Cumbria with a carload of sticks to sell to stick-dressers. He knew what we wanted. It was great material: hard, not easily broken.'

Dave continues to wander between the trees. It's a mixed wood. As well as hazel, oak and beech there's honeysuckle snaking up the trunks of smaller trees, making it an ideal habitat for dormice. But there have been no sightings of the rare mammal, which survives on flowers, nuts and fruits, this far north. Northumberland's only known colony is concealed in woodlands forty miles south.

What is of interest is that, side-by-side with the hazels, there are a few small holly trees, heavy with red berries. Do they herald a hard winter, as folklore would claim? Dave is doubtful. 'There're always plenty of berries on the holly bushes these days, but we don't seem to get the hard winters we used to,' he says. 'Maybe it's another of them old wives' tales.' But hollies aren't prized just for their berries. Heavier than hazel, they make strong sticks. With their knobbly bark they're not to everyone's taste, but a good holly stick is a work of art. On this occasion, however, there are no holly sticks to satisfy Dave's requirements and, with the breeze getting up, he sets off for home with a handful of hazels, pleased with his foray into the wood. Restlessly quartering the ground behind him, Nap and Scott follow their master.

If you know where to look in the wood, it's evident that the bushes have been shorn of a few shoots. But there is no risk that they will be permanently damaged. Hazel has extraordinary powers of regeneration. In the days when coppicing was commonplace hazel woods were cropped on a rotation to ensure a constant supply of rods and poles. It's no different from garden pruning: growth follows the knife.

The cold has permeated the old stone building where Dave has his workshop and his breath comes out in clouds as he gets to work on yet another stick, the latest in a long line going back many years. All around him is the paraphernalia of crook-making: a cast-iron pan for boiling water to soften horns sits on the stone flags; propped against the cobweb-festooned walls are bundles of maturing hazel; laid out on the workbench is an assortment of rasps and files and gripped in the vice is a horn.

It's soon clear why the cold isn't going to bother Dave. The horn has been boiled for a couple of hours and then squeezed in the vice to iron out its natural spiral. Now it's time to bend it to the shape he wants. In days gone by shepherds would leave their hills in summer and travel to the village blacksmith's shop where they would borrow the smith's tools and vice to 'set' a few horns until they were approximately the shape of a crook's head. Shepherds who lived too far from a blacksmith would resort to heating their rams' horns in the embers of a dying fire or holding them over the chimney of an oil lamp when they were trying to straighten out the curves. But when Dave needs a more precise source of heat all he needs to do is switch on an electric paint stripper. The hot air, directed on to small areas of the horn, softens it enough to allow him to keep bending it. It's a delicate balance: if too much heat is applied the horn becomes brittle, too little and it won't bend. Reheating is possible, so long as a horn is not scorched or over-heated.

Obtaining horns has become harder and harder in recent times. The best horns come mainly from rams, the older the better. In years gone by rams were turned out onto the hills at the end of their active lives and left to grow old gracefully. When they died shepherds would cut off the horns and keep them for making crooks. There was a ready supply, both for themselves and their friends. Gradually, however, farmers started to send more and more of their geriatric rams to fat-sheep sales. There they were bought by wholesale butchers who had outlets for the meat from such animals but who weren't particularly interested in what happened to their horns. So the main source began to dry up.

Then there was another blow. When Bovine Spongiform Encephalopathy (BSE) was first diagnosed in cattle in 1986 no one imagined that, as well as sending shockwaves through farming and the food industry, it would cast a shadow over the age-old practice of stick carving. But as efforts increased to prevent the spread of the disease any animal product which might carry the infectious agent came under increasing scrutiny. And that included horns. In 1996 the government ruled that, after slaughter, sheep and goats' heads – with the exception of the tongue – constituted a potential risk and must be destroyed. At a stroke, it seemed that stick carvers would be robbed of their raw material so they mounted a campaign to preserve their craft.

Three years later, just as it appeared that the British Government might relent, agriculture officials in Brussels launched a separate bid to prevent horns from goats and sheep being used in stick carving, again because of fears about the possible spread of BSE. A David-and-Goliath battle ensued, with a small group of craftsmen from the United Kingdom pitted against the might of the European Commission.

It didn't look very hopeful, but after lengthy discussions the craftsmen were eventually given permission to carry on as before. It had looked as though they would all have to be licensed and submit their premises to regular inspections by health and safety officials. But the craftsmen argued such a system would be impossible to police, since most of them fashioned their sticks in draughty sheds at the bottom of the garden or in dingy outhouses. So the powers-that-be gave in. Under sections 13, 14 and 40 of the Animal By-Products Regulations 2003 and Article 18 of Regulation (EC) number 1774/2002 it was agreed that the Minister of Agriculture would give approval to any premises set up to 'produce walking sticks and other craft products from antlers or horn'. It was even agreed that the carvers could use cattle or buffalo horn originating from outside the UK, so long as they kept a record of where they obtained it.

It still leaves the craftsmen with practical difficulties surrounding the procurement of horns from abattoirs. For welfare reasons it's illegal to remove them before slaughter, and quite right too. But because of the conveyor-belt nature of the slaughtering process it's often difficult to obtain them afterwards. So the likelihood is that horns will continue to become hard to find.

All kinds of horn can be used for decorated crooks, although deer antlers are not popular because they don't respond to heat. The finest horn is considered to come from a Dorset Horn ram, but these are rare. Despite the name, most Dorset Horns are bred as polled (hornless) animals and finding one with horns is difficult. Hill breeds of sheep such as Swaledale, Welsh Mountain and Blackface provide ideal horns for sticks.

It's an unusual choice, but Dave has decided to make a stick head using a horn from a Cheviot billy goat. For more than 200 years these wild goats have roamed the nearby hills in small flocks and because they never shed their horns, the billies often have a spectacular set. Indeed, over their lifetime, the horns can grow to more than 70 centimetres in length. From time to time it's deemed necessary to cull a few of these feral beasts, which gives crook carvers an opportunity to try their hand at something different. Some find goat horns a bit too flaky to work with but Dave likes this particular sample. It's an attractive mixture of black and blue-grey and is proving pleasantly malleable. He hasn't decided yet what decoration will adorn the stick, but there's every likelihood it will be a sheepdog – Dave's emblem.

This shepherd's hobby is known as stick 'dressing', and the term is well-chosen. For, in a craftsman's hands, a stick is transformed. All kinds of decorations are carved to adorn sticks made today. But it wasn't always such a creative activity. Sticks in the past were plain and simple, the only embellishment being a thistle on the nose of a crook made in Scotland, or made for a Scot. In the summer of 1933, two stick whittlers from the Coquet valley in Northumberland, George Snaith and Ned Henderson, each carved a brown trout on the handles of sticks exhibited at Thropton Agricultural Show. They are credited with saving the dressed stick – and turning it into an art form.

Back in the 1930s the materials used by stick-dressers were rudimentary. The design was burned on the horn using heated nails and a pair of pliers, and dye to colour it was made from herbs growing in the hedgerows. As an example of a cost-nothing solution to one of the more time-consuming aspects of stick-dressing Dave Baxter can remember seeing the shepherds of his youth using pieces of glass to file down their dressed horns and give them a perfect finish.

George Snaith and Ned Henderson's trout sticks were the start of a trend, but fashions didn't alter very quickly. Wilf Laidler, secretary of the Border Stick Dressers Association, has written an account of the association's growth since it was founded in 1951 and interesting reading it makes too. It seems that even as recently as the 1950s fancy sticks were just trout and thistle sticks – nothing more elaborate. And show categories consisted simply of neck and leg crooks, market sticks and ladies' sticks.

That was all to change, thanks to the imagination and skill of one of the most famous of the country's stick-dressers, the late Norman Tulip. His designs were intricate, with much of the inspiration coming from wildlife. The first man to fashion a horn into a lobster – on a stick dedicated to his friends in a nearby fishing village – and the pioneer of many other intricate designs, he reckoned it took 300 to 400 hours to make an ornamental stick.

Norman came originally from the wild, heather-clad hills of the North Tyne valley. As a young man he moved to a lowland farm at Rennington, near Alnwick in Northumberland, but he always remembered the shepherds he met as a boy and their skills at making sticks. Intent on learning more about stick-dressing from the acknowledged master of the craft he called one day at the isolated farm where George Snaith lived. George was notoriously secretive about his work, but Norman thought he'd give him a try.

He tapped at the door, which eventually opened a few inches. A gruff voice asked him what he wanted. When Norman explained the reason for his visit he was told to go away and make some new sticks.

'Come back when you think you've got something to show me,' the voice growled.

Wilf Laidler takes up the story. 'Well, there was a determination about Norman Tulip. He was a lovely, gentle man in many ways, he never had a bad word for anyone. But he wasn't easily put off. And a few months later there he was standing at George Snaith's back door once more with a couple of sticks. He knocked, and again it opened – the same six inches. A hand reached out and took hold of the sticks, and shut the door in Norman's face.'

After what seemed like hours, the door opened again. It was George, who said: 'Young man, I think you have talent, there's no doubt about that. And I'll show you everything I know. But that's on one condition: you must never sell a stick.'

Norman replied: 'If I get good enough I'll keep that promise. If I don't, I'll just pack it up.'

Quite why George Snaith extracted the pledge no one knows, but Norman kept it all his life. Even when times were hard, he never sold a stick. 'When you spend a few hundred hours on a stick, what's a few pound notes in your pocket?' he would say.

He wrote that one of the most important aspects of crook making was to get the right balance between the size and weight of the shank and the size and weight of the horn so that the stick, in the parlance of stick-dressers, was 'clever' to hold.

Norman's creations were so beautiful that he received recognition from the very top. His sticks were considered good enough to be presented to the Queen and the Duke of Edinburgh. And in his memory 37 of his best sticks are exhibited in the dining room at Alnwick Castle, home of the Duke of Northumberland.

Not all sticks are used for practical purposes; some are used away from the farm. When they're visiting their local agricultural show or having a day out at the auction mart most shepherds feel incomplete without a stick. In those sort of places crooks are for propping yourself up on. At least that's how they always seem to be used as the shepherds relax, supported by their sticks, beside the sheep pens, their eyes narrowing as they assess the animals on show. Those particular crooks are their favourite ones, often carrying the owner's name and the name of the place he hails from. The maker's initials, or his trademark (Norman Tulip's was a reef knot) are usually marked on the horn.

But of course, crooks do have many practical uses. Like all sticks, they help to steady a person's foothold when they're walking on rough terrain. They're essential for catching and holding a sheep, especially out in the fields. And they can be used to probe deep drifts of snow for sheep which may have been buried in a winter storm. They are the shepherd's assistant.

'A farmer I knew used to tell a story to illustrate the importance of crooks,' says Wilf Laidler. 'Sometimes visitors would come to the farm and express scepticism about the farmer's methods of handling his sheep. "Well," he'd say, "if you can catch a sheep without any help you can have it," but no one ever could. You need a good dog and a stick.'

In his workshop Dave busies himself with fashioning the goat's horn into a stick handle. He's already chosen a good hazel shank and is preparing to 'marry' the two by drilling holes in the shank head and the horn's heel and gluing in a steel rod to connect the two. This should give the crook the strength to cope with all jobs – and in all weathers.

'I've always enjoyed working with tools,' Dave says. 'I picked up a lot from old stick-dressers when I was young, and it spurred me on. I've learned a lot myself, making mistakes and trying to correct them. It's been something I've really enjoyed.'

Fancy sticks intended for stick-dressing classes at agricultural shows must be made from a single piece of horn without any extra pieces stuck on. This is what tests the stick-dresser. Dave says: 'The best plain stick I've seen recently was the champion at Yetholm Show over the Border. Made by Gordon Flintoft, a stick-dresser from Yorkshire, it was a Wiltshire horn, from a Wiltshire ram, and it was a terrific stick.' The winner of the fancy stick category at Yetholm was Lawrence Batey, of Acomb near Hexham, who's still carving sticks at the age of 90.

'Just goes to prove that there's nowt that can harm you in carving sticks,' grins Wilf Laidler in a clear reference to the battles he's fought to preserve stick-dressing from the attentions of the government and the European Union.

Evening classes in stick-dressing are held at half-a-dozen different places in the north-east of England, and there are stick-whittlers' associations all over the country. Fewer shepherds are making fancy sticks, however. The older ones are dying out and the young ones aren't interested. But overall the numbers of stick-dressers is increasing as people from other walks of life take up the hobby.

So how far back in history do shepherds' crooks go? Victorian illustrations depicting Palestinian shepherds in biblical times show the bearded flock-keepers holding crooks. But that may have been artistic licence. According to the Bible the Palestinian shepherd was kitted out with two pieces of equipment used for self-preservation rather than catching sheep: 'Thy rod and thy staff they comfort me'(Psalm 23, Verse 4). The rod was a short club which shepherds used to protect them from robbers, wild animals and snakes, and the staff was a tall stick, forked at the top, which was used as a walking stick. Quite how the crook became the symbol of Church leaders isn't clear.

The crook as we would recognise it is said to have been an English development in the Middle Ages but until the 16th century there is little recorded evidence of its use. The poet Michael Drayton (1563-1631) noticed that the swains in his neighbourhood had crooks, and were interested in decorating them: 'Shepherds are proud of their sharp hooks, carved out with many a strange device.'

By the 18th century the design of crooks had become more or less standardised. In England, leg crooks became popular, although details of their design differed from area to area. Made of iron by the local blacksmith to the shepherd's own specifications they were fitted by a socket to a wooden shaft between three and five feet in length. These crooks were used to grab a sheep by the hind leg, just above the hock. The dimensions of a leg crook (or cleek as it was known as in the North of England) were very precise to avoid damaging – or even breaking – a sheep's back leg. The 'loop' of the crook was under two inches wide and the mouth even narrower, making it difficult for a sheep to slip away.

Metal neck crooks were extensively used in flocks too. They were about four inches wide at the mouth and, like leg crooks, often had a decorative whorl on the end. In some places the status of the shepherd was indicated by his stick: one whorl on the end signified an under-shepherd, two whorls a head shepherd.

As farmers sought to earn more from their sheep's wool during the 19th century they built rudimentary dipping baths to wash the animals in, especially on farms where there was no convenient river or stream to drive the animals through. The evolution of dipping sticks to handle sheep being dipped took place at the same time. They sported two loops facing in opposite directions, one with its mouth towards the shepherd for lifting a sheep's head clear of the water and one facing away from the user to immerse the animal in the water. To provide greater leverage, the handles were up to ten feet in length. Examples of these crooks can be seen in museums of country life.

Shepherds have always set themselves apart from other agricultural workers and this was particularly the case at hiring fairs in the 19th century, where shepherds would carry the symbol of their work, a crook, as they waited on the streets of their local market town for someone to come up and offer them a job.

∾

Clothing

How to stay dry in the rain which drenches the high ground inhabited by Britain's sheep is something which constantly challenges the men and women who tend those animals. The lobby in Stewart and Gwen's cottage is crammed with a vast range of outdoor gear and footwear, all of it warm and waterproof. It is a veritable shrine to Goretex. Lined up on the floor are pairs of wellingtons in different colours, lightweight boots of the kind endorsed by athletes and mountaineers, and heavy work boots. On the walls are hooks festooned with fleeces, oilskins, anoraks, cagoules, overtrousers and thick jackets. Scarves and gloves peep out from half-closed drawers. It's all a far cry from the garments worn by shepherds in days gone by.

The biggest change has taken place in the south of England. Shepherds working on the Downs in the 18th and 19th centuries wore a traditional costume which was considered to be practical, but which also made it easy to recognise the wearer's rank. The main – and most familiar – garment was the smock. This basic overall was usually homespun from a long-lasting material such as hemp or flax. It was generously cut to allow freedom of movement and reached down to well below the knee. Most were identical front and back, and the fact that they were reversible helped to prolong their life. Nearly all boasted wide floppy collars.

In damp weather some shepherds would pull on an old smock brushed over with boiled oil and lamp blackening to make it waterproof. As an extra layer of protection when carrying an ailing ewe or poorly lamb they sometimes wore an old sack across their shoulders.

All smocks were gathered at the chest and cuffs. This was done with a smocking stitch which varied from garment to garment. Most smock sleeves were also gathered at the shoulder with the same ornate stitch. Between the gathering panel on the chest and the sleeve was an area known as the box. This and the collar were often intricately embroidered with designs reflecting the owner's trade. Details such as crooks and sheep were regularly worked into the design. The colour of smocks varied from locality to locality (Kendal Green, Coventry Blue, Kent Grey and so on) with white being the most common, despite its obviously impractical nature in an outdoor garment worn by someone working with sheep, often in muddy conditions.

Under their smocks shepherds wore linen or woollen shirts and corduroy breeches either tied above the ankle with twine or combined with short worsted stockings or leather leggings. Many smocks had voluminous poachers' pockets for storing shepherds' tools or their midday snack.

Some shepherds sported a mushroom-shaped hat to which a tuft of wool was pinned as a badge of office. When a shepherd was recruited at a hiring fair the tuft was removed and replaced with a ribbon tied in a bow.

Writing in the 1870s, Thomas Hardy remarked that fashions didn't seem to alter much in the shepherding world. He had noticed that the 'cut' of a gaiter and the embroidery on a smock was the same as it had been 100 years previously. Nevertheless, the wearing of the smock as a working overall began to die out as the 19th century wore on and few were worn later than 1890, apart from on special occasions such as harvest festivals and sheep fairs.

While smocks were the traditional garment favoured by shepherds in the south of England, sheepskins were popular in the north and in Scotland shepherds took to wearing a plaid and bonnet. The plaid was a single piece of cloth woven from the finest wool. It was wrapped round the wearer's body and shoulders and held in place by a buckle, from this hung a bell, a lamp and sometimes a small keg. The contents of the latter depended on the shepherd's taste and the size of his wallet. Ale or cider were consumed during the milder weather, but in the winter months shepherds generally favoured the inner warmth provided by a tot of whisky or some powerful concoction brewed in an illicit still.

One legacy of the clan system in Scotland was that the number of colours in the plaid varied according to the rank of the bearer. The chief's plaid was a rainbow of seven colours, four colours were permitted for lesser nobilities and just two, black and white, for the hired shepherd. Despite its lowly connotations the black-and-white check became fashionable in the early part of the 19th century, first among the aristocracy (one enthusiast was the writer Sir Walter Scott) and later with the middle classes. The mill town of Galashiels in the Borders became famous throughout the world as the centre for making the checked cloth known as 'shepherd's plaid' or 'shepherd's check'.

Anyone who might be interested in finding out more about shepherds' plaids will find it worthwhile contacting a keeper of rural life at Beamish Museum in County Durham where some beautiful examples are stored in the collection of items from our rural past.

Waterproof clothes are vital for people whose days are mostly spent out of doors. But keeping the upper body dry is just part of the struggle; boots are equally important. For, as all shepherds know, tramping over the moors with cold or sore feet can soon become an uncomfortably depressing experience.

Until the 1920s every town and village had its shoemaker. People awoke to the tramp-tramp-tramp of men going to work in their hob-nail boots, and they were familiar with the clatter of clogs as children scampered along the streets to school. In the country, clogs were worn by adults and children alike. But for shepherds expected to march resolutely up steep hillsides in search of their sheep there was a special form of foot-covering, the tacketty boot.

Stewart has vivid memories of buying his first pair of 'hill buits', as the Scots term them, in 1977. It was something of a rite of passage. With his herd's crook and his tacketty boots, he'd joined the select world of hill men. 'It was just after I first started work that I bought a pair of hill boots with turned up toes and tacketty soles. They cost me £28 which was a week's wages in those days. It was a lot of money, but I had to have those boots. They were what every self-respecting shepherd wore. Nowadays you could be looking at £180 to £190 for boots like that – if you could still get them. I'm not sure if anyone makes them any more.'

Leather hill boots were made by hand and had a distinctive shape. They were turned up at the front, which produced a rocking effect when walking. As the wearer headed uphill the boots propelled him forward. Shepherds swore they could eat up the miles on their rounds much faster if they wore these boots with their 'perky, upturned nose like a ferret emerging from a rabbit hole,' as one writer put it. Mind you, on smooth surfaces like the polished pavements of market towns and the icy expanse of a frozen farmyard in winter, tacketty boots lost their adhesion and gave their wearers some anxious moments.

Hill boots were available in horse hide or cow hide and there were long discussions among their devotees as to which form of leather was best. When new, they were stiff, but after being worn two or three times, during which the stitching would swell making the boot watertight, they fitted like a glove. Not being of rubber, they allowed the foot to breathe. Some claimed they were so comfortable that socks weren't needed.

Protruding from the soles were the 'tackets', round-headed steel nails. Purchasers of hill boots could choose their own pattern, but the nails were usually inserted in a double row round the rim and a half-moon shape on the ball of the foot. It was these nails which gave the boots their grip. Sometimes a shepherd whose beat was a heather moor had strips of copper fitted to the toes to prevent the wiry heather stems from unpicking the stitching. Long-lasting steel heel-plates helped boots to have a long life. Stewart swears his would still be in use if they hadn't been destroyed in the fire which raged through his house in 1990.

They may have been durable, but hill boots were heavy. Depending on the measurements (the largest anyone can remember was a size 18) they weighed roughly six pounds each, which was rather like having two kilos of sugar strapped to each ankle. By the end of a day spent herding sheep over bogs and burns on the far-flung expanses of the farm, shepherds knew they'd been on a strenuous hike. Many had two pairs of boots, one for current use and the other stewing in castor oil while the leather recuperated from weeks of hard work. Living in remote places, shepherds were usually unable to collect the hill boots they'd ordered so the boots were delivered by post, in many cases (because of their weight) in two separate parcels.

Established in 1905, Thomas Rogerson and Sons of Innerleithen, Selkirkshire and Rothbury, Northumberland were among the foremost suppliers of hill boots. A descendent of the founder, Ian Rogerson, has fond memories of the family exhibiting their wares at agricultural shows in Pennine towns and villages in the 1950s and 1960s, a time when the leather hill boot was still the shepherd's only choice of footwear. 'They were the most popular things we sold,' he recalls. 'Faithful customers would come back time after time to see what you had in the way of boots. You felt it was a trade that would last for ever.'

It's not clear at what point the popularity of the hill boot began to wane, but when climbers conquered Everest in 1953 wearing boots with 'commando' soles, customers wanted something similar. Soon tackets became scarce, oiled thread was in short supply and firms no longer made leather laces. 'It had a domino effect', Ian says. 'Steel heel-plates were hard to come by, and then eventually the bootmakers themselves began to die out.'

By the late 1960s, Rogersons had sold their last tacketty boot, but Stewart had managed to track down another footwear supplier who still had a few left a decade later.

∾

Counting Sheep

It has many of the ingredients of a scene from days gone by: sheep waiting in groups, people clustered around the pens, shepherds shouting and dogs barking. If it wasn't for the fact that it's mid-winter rather than mid-summer it could be a sheep-shearing day 100 years ago, so great is the number of helpers. However, this is Blindburn in the twenty-first century, not the 1900s. And what's happening is that the ewes are being scanned to see if they're pregnant and if so, how many lambs they're carrying. It's one of the aspects of sheep production where new technology has transformed traditional husbandry. Yet at the same time, it remains one of those jobs where many hands make light work.

As well as Judith Ridley, the farmer at Blindburn, her son Matthew, and their shepherds Gwen and Stewart Wallace, there are four shepherds from neighbouring farms and two students from agricultural college. Everyone from the valley has rallied round and they are all united in the same aim: to funnel sheep through the scanning procedure as quickly as possible.

Although families have all other mod cons, mains electricity is still not available in the Upper Coquet valley. When considering a scheme to connect the area to the national grid the planning authorities insisted that cables must run underground rather than be carried on posts, which would, in their view, spoil the appearance of the landscape. But the cost of burying the power line was too great for residents to pay, so they all rely on generators. It's one of those machines which, throbbing quietly in its barn, provides the power for scanning at Blindburn.

From a large gathering area sheep are herded in batches through a series of holding pens until they are manoeuvred into a race. Along this narrow channel they move, one by one, into a specially-designed handling crate where they are scanned for a few seconds before being released. The scanning operator, David

Eames, relaxes on an old car seat next to the crate, almost at eye level with the ewes as they pass by him. From this position he can reach under a sheep and run his ultrasound probe across its abdomen. The image it transmits appears on a small screen in front of him.

'Pregnancy scanning in sheep was "borrowed" from human healthcare 25 years ago,' he explains, 'and it's one of the things which has revolutionised hill farming. It's similar to what happens with women in hospital, using an ultrasound scanner to detect the unborn foetus. The sound waves from the scanner go into the ewe and bounce back off the skeletal image of the lamb or lambs, and then you see the images on the screen.'

The scanner's skill lies in analysing the shadowy picture on the screen and detecting how many lambs the ewe is carrying. As each goes through he presses a button on an electronic counter and the results are continuously updated on the screen under the headings of 'empty', 'one', 'two', 'three' or 'four'. It's extremely unlikely that any sheep, particularly a hill sheep, will be carrying quadruplets and triplets are very rare indeed among Blackface ewes. But the remaining information is highly useful to hill farmers because it enables them to concentrate on sheep that really need extra attention. If a ewe is empty ('geld' or 'yeld' as it's known in the North and Scotland) she's usually fattened up and sold straight away, although 'gimmers' (in their first year as breeding females) that are not pregnant at their first scanning are often retained in the flock and given a second chance. Ewes carrying one lamb are returned to the hirsel they came from and allowed to continue their lives with a minimal amount of supervision. But ewes known to be pregnant with twins can be split off from the rest and moved to better ground where they will be given extra feed to help sustain two lambs, and will receive greater surveillance at lambing time.

So that everyone who works on the farm knows which sheep are pregnant, David calls out the result as he scans them and Matthew marks the animals on the back of their necks, one colour for 'empty' and one for twins. The assumption is that the rest will be carrying singles.

The reason for trying to scan ewes as fast as possible is to make best use of the scanner's time. The season is short and he has to work long hours to make it pay. Sheep are pregnant for about 150 days and David prefers to scan them at about 80 days from the start of tupping time. This gives him a scanning 'window' of about 40 days.

The set-up at Blindburn, coupled with the number of helpers, make scanning a speedy and efficient process. But conditions vary from farm to farm and at some places progress can be slow. 'The most I've ever done was 400 sheep an hour, but in some situations I might scan as few as 100,' he says. 'It all depends. The average is about 250.'

Determining how many lambs the womb is holding isn't always easy. 'Many things can affect the picture on the screen. The age of the lamb; how far in lamb the ewe is; how fat the sheep is, because overweight sheep develop a layer of fat over the belly and are harder to scan. Another factor is what the sheep has eaten in the previous 24 hours. If it's been on concentrates, silage, hay or bulky food, it can create a lot of gas in the stomach and that can affect the quality of the picture.'

At least the scanner spends his time working indoors. 'Obviously it's more pleasant for me if the sheep are dry; but if they're wet, well, you just put up with that. As a whole, the weather as such doesn't really affect the scanning, except when there's a really heavy snowfall and the farmers and their shepherds can't gather the sheep in.'

David charges between 35p and 50p per sheep, depending on how many sheep he has to scan. 'The more you scan the cheaper it becomes,' he says. 'It doesn't really matter what breed they are, because sheep are all basically the same, it's really a question of numbers.'

David's life is a busy one and his entrepreneurial spirit is typical of that shown by many of today's agricultural contractors. He runs his own farm in the picturesque Trough of Bowland in Lancashire and spends the spring lambing his flock of 600 ewes. In summer he packs his shears and travels all over the North of England, working on farms as a clipper. Then in the winter he's on the road with his ultrasound equipment, diagnosing pregnancies in sheep. What he really enjoys about working as a contractor is that it provides him with the opportunity to meet people. 'Scanning's a hard job, with long hours,' he says. 'So is clipping. But you go to so many different places in so many different landscapes, and you meet so many great characters. That's what makes it all special for me.'

ༀ

Storms

When the winter time is stormy and the drifts are piling high
He will never fail to take a risk, though in the snow might die
For to seek the sheep into a stell where they may softly lie,
That's the canny shepherd laddie of the hills.

We wanted to film the Cheviot Hills in snow, but we got a bit more than we bargained for. At Alwinton the road was still passable, but by the time we reached the next settlement, Barrow Mill, the wheels of the car were struggling to grip. The cameraman had a set of snow chains, but for some reason they didn't fit. We had to turn back.

There's no signal for mobile phones in the upper Coquet valley so I prised open the door of the public phonebox in Alwinton and dialled Stewart's number. 'The snow's too thick,' I said when he picked up the phone, 'we can't get through.'

It's a reflection of Stewart's generous nature that he calmly replied: 'I'll come and get you. It'll be nae bother.' It's ten miles up the valley road to Blindburn, and it was an hour before the headlights of Stewart's jeep appeared in the swirling snow. Within a few minutes we'd loaded the camera equipment and were heading back up the valley at a snail's pace, grateful for the four-wheel-drive steadiness of the vehicle as it barged through the drifts. 'It'll take a while but I'll get you there,' promised Stewart, unflappable as ever. 'Whether you'll be able to get back is another matter.'

Snow comes in different forms. In this January blizzard it was a light powder which, whipped by a strong North wind, filled the hollows and formed strange shapes at the side of the road. It had a wilful unpredictability about it. It was snow you treated warily.

Blizzards shouldn't come as a surprise to shepherds, for as well as up-to-the-minute weather forecasts there are all sorts of country sayings which predict snow. It's said that hill sheep have an instinctive dread of a coming storm and if a shepherd meets his flock coming down from the hill tops on a winter's night he knows a storm is brewing. It's also claimed that old sheep eat greedily before a storm and sparingly before a thaw.

The devastating effects of a fierce snow storm are well remembered by hill folk who lived through the winters of 1947, 1953, 1963 and 1979. The trouble with sheep is that they instinctively turn their backs to a storm and are forcibly propelled by the wind to the nearest place of shelter. With any luck this may be one of the 'stells' mentioned earlier, but on open moorland it's often a cleft in the hillside or a deep burn, and in no time at all the gully is full of snow and the sheep are buried. There are tales of ewes surviving for weeks in ice 'igloos', sometimes by eating each other's wool, but more often than not the animals are smothered.

It's not just the immediate losses caused by a snow storm, it's the consequential damage. Sheep that do manage to come through are often in very poor condition and as a result lamb crops are low. Mary Carruthers, Dave's employer, recalls that when it came to clipping the family's flock in the summer following the 1947 storm, shearers found that the ewes' fleeces, normally greasy, were completely dry and brittle.

Sheep usually cope with harsh weather by scratching away at the ground to expose some vegetation that they can nibble, and by getting a bite from the 'bulls' snouts', tufts of grass which poke out of the snow. But in 1947 the snow was just too deep. In many places it piled up in such huge drifts that it was level with the tops of the telegraph poles. When the postman finally got through to remote Cheviot farms after they'd been cut off for 19 weeks he walked right over the gates without even realising they were there, so deep was the snow.

Sometimes a spring storm can cause havoc. Shepherds in the North of England and Scotland can well remember the storm which blew up on April 24th in the spring of 1982. Fields full of lambs disappeared under deep drifts. 'There had been severe winds and the snow was piled up against the walls,' one recalls. 'It took a lot of people completely by surprise.' As happens on these occasions sheepdogs can pinpoint the spot where sheep are entombed and by poking their crooks through the drifts shepherds are able to accurately locate the buried animals. 'When we dug down we found twins lying side by side like Christmas crackers in a box, still breathing,' Stewart remembers. 'I'll never forget that. We got most of them out alive and then, being spring, the snow melted quite quickly.'

Luckily for us the snow flurries abate and we can film Stewart and Gwen feeding rams at Blindburn. The farm's Blackface ewes, however, remain far away on their hirsels and with the outlook so unsettled, we decide not to try and film them on the tops. They are well looked after, however, with feedblocks to lick for nutrition. And each hill on the farm has a hut where hay bales are stored in case of an emergency. If there's a heavy fall of snow the sheep make their way to the hut where they can be fed by the shepherds. 'It has to be really bad before we do that,' Stewart says. 'Most of the time the sheep have to fend for themselves as best they can. They're born and bred on the hills and used to the hill weather.'

The light is starting to go and you can feel more snow is coming. It's back into the jeep again to attempt the road out of the valley. Slowly Stewart picks his way along the narrow road, bumping through drifts and slipping on patches of ice. At last we see the lights of Alwinton again. We head off in our car, knowing Stewart has another testing trip back to Blindburn. 'I'll just take my time,' he says serenely. 'I'll get there in the end.'

◠

The Shepherds' Supper

They don't weigh as much as the Blackface rams he's manhandled in the sheep pens over the years and certainly they don't struggle as much, but the beer barrels Stewart's hauling up the steps are bulky enough to give his back the occasional twinge. It's a Friday afternoon in early March and the final preparations are under way for the annual shepherds' supper, a tradition which, despite the decline in shepherds, is still clinging on in a few upland areas of the country.

Coming from north of the Border, Stewart prefers to use the Scottish abbreviation 'herd' when talking about shepherds. To him, it's a 'herds' supper'. But whatever the name, the ingredients are straightforward: a slap-up meal, a few snatches of music, plenty to drink and the company of fellow countrymen. As he explains: 'It's really just a get-together of the hill men before lambing starts. One last chance to blow off steam before we get down to the nitty-gritty of lambing time.'

Putting on an evening of entertainment may sound simple enough, but it takes a lot of organising. Stewart's the one who does it, virtually single-handed. On winter evenings in the run-up to the supper he's on the phone booking musicians, lining up speakers and cajoling the local shepherding fraternity to venture out. 'In the old days shepherds used to go and visit each other in their cottages,' he says. 'They'd walk a long way for a drink, a game of cards and a bit of banter at the fireside. But nowadays, with the growth of television and modern transport, they don't visit each other as often as they used to. They're more inclined to go to the pub than go and see their friend over the hill.' Moreover with the advent of the breathalyser, even that's not as common as it used to be. The number of pubs in rural areas is steadily dwindling as a result.

This particular shepherds' shindig has been held in the upper Coquet valley for many decades. In the days before they had their own cars shepherds used to come on foot over the fells and stagger home in the dark, warmed by the memory of a good night out. For many years it was held in the pub at Alwinton, ten miles down the valley from Stewart's home at Blindburn. Then interest waned and for a while the event lapsed, only for it to be resuscitated by Stewart in 2002. Now it's held in the Village Hall at Harbottle, a village a couple of miles from Alwinton. The hub of the community, the hall is an ideal venue for the shepherds' bash, with a large room for the meal, space where food can be prepared and a small scullery which doubles as the bar. Crucial to the smooth running of the event are Robert Dunn, landlord of the village pub, who supplies the drinks and the glasses, and his wife Ann, who's in charge of the food.

At 7.00 pm the first guests are being dropped off at the hall and by 7.30 everyone's enjoying a drink and shaking hands with colleagues, many of whom they haven't seen for a while. The solitary nature of shepherds' jobs makes it all the more enjoyable to catch up with old friends. It's worth mentioning, though, that not all the 60 guests are shepherds. In fact only about half are directly involved in tending flocks. The rest have links with the land, either currently or in the past. Dave Baxter's here, of course. He's been to many a shepherds' supper in his time and wouldn't miss it for anything. Robert McKay can't make it this time, but his father Tom, a shepherd and noted sheep-breeder and exhibitor, is here, dapper in a dark suit. While there are some young faces, the average age of the shepherds is probably about 50.

Three parallel rows of tables, covered in white cloths, fill the room. At the top, at right angles to the tables, sit three men: Peter Stott, a farmer, who is chairman for the evening, and two guest speakers. At the moment they're quietly sipping their drinks. Their turn will come later.

Tonight the guests are all men. Women could come if they wanted to, but they prefer to let their menfolk enjoy themselves without female company for once. Gwen, in fact, is happy to be entertaining shepherds' wives and girlfriends at a small party back in her cottage at Blindburn.

In the bar, pints are being pulled and tots of whisky poured. A few bottles of alcopops sit forlornly on the counter, unwanted by this particular clientele.

The meal is served: soup, a hearty beef stew with Yorkshire pudding and new potatoes, and trifle. Plates are cleared with gusto, cigarettes are lit and guests sit back to soak up the entertainment. First out of the trap is Graham Dick, the singing shepherd who made such an impression at Rothbury Traditional Music Festival back in the summer. His repertoire is a mixture of dialect poems, Border ballads, bawdy adaptations of traditional songs and well-known Northumbrian ditties, all of them unaccompanied.

Graham concludes his set by singing a poignant account of the disasters of a lambing time on the hills, when wintry weather greets the arrival of another crop of tiny lambs. 'Some lambs will scramble to their feet, some never rise at all …' As the verses pour forth shepherds in the audience nod their heads, for the song echoes their determination to keep as many lambs alive while the elements conspire against them:

'Thank God it doesn't happen like that every year,' Graham says at the end, as the applause dies down.

Another shepherd, Peter Tweedie, steps up to keep the music going with tunes from his set of lowland pipes. Peter's patch, on the Scottish side of the Cheviot Hills, 'marches' (borders) the land on Blindburn and sometimes he meets up with the shepherds from the English side for a chat on top of the mountain.

The evening's first speaker is Lt. Col. Richard Cross, former commandant of the Otterburn Ranges. He's a well-known figure in these parts: most of the shepherds in the hall work on farms on the military training area. Colonel Cross regales the guests with the story about a shepherd from the Coquet Valley who was looking for a new dog. He called in to look at one being offered for sale by a collie breeder in the Berwick district. After the dog's owner had displayed its talents, which hadn't wholly impressed the shepherd, the owner said 'Well, just watch this.' He sent the dog out across the River Tweed and the dog walked on the water. When he got to the other side, the owner said: 'Watch again'. And the dog walked back across the water and came up to him. The owner said: 'Well, what do you think of it?' The shepherd thought for a moment and then replied: 'I'm afraid it'll not do me. It can't swim.'

After proposing a toast to the shepherds, Colonel Cross gives way to Andrew Charleton whose guitar spills out a cascade of Northumbrian tunes. Then up steps another entertainer, Mungo Riddell, who has the guests splitting their sides as he tells one joke after another, most of them unrepeatable. Then, strapping on his piano accordion, Mungo sets their feet tapping with a string of traditional Scottish tunes.

Mungo started his life on the land by working for eight years on a farm in Berwickshire before joining a firm selling tractors and farm machinery at Haddington in the Lothians. In 1990 the company started a new branch at Alnwick in Northumberland and Mungo moved there. Today he sells farmers biological treatments for silage. His hobby is competitive ploughing and in the autumn he and his young sons can be found with his vintage Nuffield tractor and two match ploughs, turning the rich Scottish soil at ploughing competitions in the Borders.

Mungo ends his spot with a lovely, lilting waltz. It's called, appropriately, 'Furrow's End'.

The evening is drawing to an end but there's time for one more speaker to reminisce about sheep farming in days gone by. Farmer Michael Peters says there's a bit of him that wishes he could turn back the clock to the days when clipping days were great get-togethers. 'The gooseberry pies were so good at dinner-time that no one clipped a sheep till tea-time, they were that full of food,' he remembers.

He recollects a day half a century ago when he passed two shepherds leaning on the fence and chatting to each other at Carter Bar, the spot at the western end of the Cheviots where the A68 crosses from England into Scotland. When he returned almost three hours later, he noticed the shepherds were still there, talking languidly and clearly in no hurry to leave. 'Everyone seemed to have much more time in those days,' he says. 'There was great fellowship in the hills.'

A full moon is shining as the guests spill out of the village hall.

The musicians pack up their instruments and head for home. Another herds' supper is over and it's been a memorable night. But how many more years will it be held?

Postscript

*H*owever content they may be in their job, most people ask themselves from time to time whether they shouldn't be thinking of making a change. In Stewart's case, he'd been happy working as a shepherd at Blindburn for 20 years when he began to consider setting himself a fresh challenge. At the beginning of February 2004 he announced that he'd accepted a new position as shepherd on a farm in south-west Scotland and that he and Gwen would be leaving on March 20th. For their employer Judith, losing her two shepherds a month before lambing time presented her with a challenge, too. But she managed to find a lad to help her and Matthew, her son, and at the time of writing was beginning to look for full-time replacements for Stewart and Gwen, difficult though that might be in these days of declining shepherd numbers.

Stewart finds it difficult to contain his excitement about his new job, which entails working for Scotland's second largest landowner, the Duke of Buccleugh, on a 2,000-acre hill farm at Penpont near Thornhill in Dumfriesshire. 'I wanted to have a new challenge and this job gives me that,' he says. 'There's part-time work for Gwen on the estate and full-time work for me. I'll be looking after 1,000 Blackface ewes and 250 hoggs but I get all my clipping, all my dipping and all my scanning done for me.'

'I'll be sad to leave,' he admits. 'I've thoroughly enjoyed working here for the last 20 years. Neither of us are from the area, but we've been made very welcome here. As I told them all at the end of the herds' supper, it's been an honour and a privilege to work among them. Naturally, we'll make new friends in Dumfriesshire. But we'll keep our old friends in Northumberland.'

Gwen says: 'I've loved living in Northumberland. We've mixed in well with the community. Even though it's a small country place there's lots going on. You get involved with the committees for the agricultural shows and those sorts of things. If the people in Dumfriesshire are as nice as they are in Northumberland I'll be happy.'

The Wallaces have been particularly popular members of the upper Coquetdale community. Proof of that came in the farewell gifts they received from three local organisations. They were beautiful paintings of the valley by a local artist, all of them different views. There was also a nice moment when Stewart and Gwen popped in to the inn in the village for their last game of dominoes before leaving the area. Dave Baxter was there with a rugged-looking lambing stick he'd made for Stewart as a goodbye gift. 'It's for good luck in the future,' Dave explained. As shepherds do, Stewart balled his fist and passed it through the crook on the head of the stick. There was just enough room for his fist – which means there will be just enough width for the crook to clasp a sheep round its neck. 'Aye,' said Stewart, touched by Dave's gesture. 'Just right for the lambing.'

At Linshiels, Dave's job as shepherd has been taken by Robert McKay. It's an appropriate choice because Robert knows the farm. He worked there with Dave as a lad, and often helped out at busy times. For Dave, meanwhile, retirement hasn't meant putting his feet up: he's still buying, breeding and training sheepdogs, and looks after a few pedigree Blackface sheep of his own. And in April 2004 he was back on familiar ground, working for a few weeks as a 'lambing man' on a hill farm in Scotland – and making use of all the skills he'd learned in 50 years in the Borders. As the old adage goes: once a shepherd, always a shepherd.

Little was Dave to know, however, that his life was about to be changed. A few days after his return from Scotland, the unthinkable happened. May 16th, 2004, was a warm spring day and the countryside was looking its best. But Mona felt unable to appreciate it. She complained of being unwell, took refuge in her home thinking the feeling would pass, but sadly died. She was only 64. All those bereaved – particularly Dave and their children – were left with a sense of shock at the suddenness of her departure.

A sadness for me is that Mona never got to read about her husband's life as a hill shepherd, or see him and his sheepdogs featured in a series of programmes on television.

She will be greatly missed.

As I wrote in the acknowledgements at the beginning of this book, it was the shepherds and their families – people like Mona – who made us feel welcome in their midst over the two years that we spent recording 'The Last Shepherds'.

The final verse from The Canny Shepherd Laddie sums up the friendly reception we got.

> *Now if you have gone amongst them as I've done for 50 year*
> *No kinder hearted folk you'll meet if you look far or near*
> *For the kettle's set a-boiling and there's cries of 'sit doon here'*
> *That's the canny shepherd laddie of the hills.*